CORN

TOP 10

GOLDENEYE

INTRODUCTION

This little book is a condensed version of Goldeneye's Cornwall Guidebook. Goldeneye have been publishing Cornwall Travel Guides in various formats for 30-years, and this is the first time a Top 10 has been identified by us. Those chosen, for the Top 10 in each category, has not been done lightly. In an Age when time is at a premium, and when the modern traveller seeks only the best, and is given to short breaks, it seems an apposite moment to publish this book. The Top 10 are included on merit, and merit alone. We gain no advertising revenue from them for appearing in this book. We do, however, welcome your feedback.

Cornwall is a County of great diversity, of strange customs and superstitions, of romantic legends and Arthurian myths. A County steeped in its own language, culture and, outlook. Remote, and cut off from the rest of Britain by the Tamar, the Cornish have developed a proud individuality and resilient independence. The close proximity to the Gulf Stream provides a warm and equable climate. The magnificent coastline, relentlessly shaped by the elements, with its contorted rocks, precipitous cliffs, deep estuaries, smugglers' coves, golden beaches and picturesque harbours, is unmatched elsewhere in England.

The landscape is haunted by countless landmarks of early man; Long Barrows, Quoits, Hill Forts and Stone Circles, and to put these into an historic perspective, the Neolithic Period gave place to the Bronze Age around 2000 BC, the Iron Age lasted from about 500 BC up to Roman times, the first 4 centuries AD.

The Cornish skyline has been shaped by the remains of chimneys and engine houses, and by ramshackle desolate buildings beside the road - the remains of a once prosperous tin and copper mining industry.

With few exceptions, Cornwall has been noted for the setting of architecture rather than architecture itself. However, there are fine examples of medieval fortresses and elegant country houses surrounded by spacious gardens, as well as an increasing number of more modern buildings; Truro College, the Tremough Campus at Penryn, and the RNLI Lifeboat Station at Trevose Head.

Whilst working on this book I looked at the range of environmentally conscious hotels, B&Bs, and dining pubs, not to mention the traditional artisans who work with natures' produce to create beautiful pieces of art. It occurred to me that many of the places I have selected have strong and positive environmental practices. Most of the eateries, from pubs to country house hotels use locally produced food with low food miles, thereby supporting local producers, and a lot of the places to stay focus their business on protecting their beautiful surroundings for generations to come. It is surely no surprise that the inhabitants of such a beautiful County as Cornwall would want to use its resources but use them in a way that prolongs them rather than depletes them. With nearly 300 miles of coastland virtually wrapping around the whole county, it is little wonder that so much of the area has turned to the sea for its influences. Here, the skills of the fisherman, the farmer, and the chef, come to the fore. Given the natural austerity of the farmland in the area, Cornish farmers have worked with nature to farm the livestock and crops that work with the natural vagaries of the area.

So, in short, you can assume that most of the places featured in this book use local food producers even though I may not say so. And, although not all hotels can be considered eco-friendly, many B&Bs in this book are just that (as well as being super places to stay).

I believe Cornwall to be a truly magical holiday destination, whether you have a weekend, a week, are alone, with friends or family. Whether, you have a particular interest in surfing, gardens, history, or simple hedonism. There is no shortage of options for you. Take a deep breath of sea air, shrug off your working persona and pretend you live here for a couple of days…I promise you'll feel better.

William Fricker
Buckland Barton, June 2013

Bodinnick Ferry, Fowey

MAIN CENTRES

Bodmin. The County town of Cornwall is positioned in the centre of the county, just off the busy A30. It is worth a stop-over to explore the interesting museums, and the C15 St Petroc, the largest Parish Church in the County. It does not have the chic shops of Truro or the dramatic locations of Falmouth and Penzance. It is a quiet, country town full of history. Witness the historic prison, scene of public executions until 1862, and Protector/Keeper of the Crown Jewels in WWI. The Information Centre is set in the old Court House where the ghosts and spirits of unlucky souls foundered. A grand start-off point for the Camel Trail. Indoor swimming pool. E/C W. www.bodminlive.com or www.bodmin.gov.uk

Bude. A seaside resort first developed by the Victorians that has witnessed, of late, much resurgence, in no small part due to the popularity of surfing and beach activities. The long, extensive beaches, just a short walk from the town centre, and those to the south and north of the town, are breathtaking. The coastline demands respect and has been the scene of many shipwrecks - 80 ships were foundered, or wrecked between 1824- 74. The town abounds with the buzz of surf shops, surf hostels and cafés, and when the Low Pressure is in force the beaches are populated with black shadows, in summer, and winter. It is the most accessible of the Cornish surf resorts. Canal carnival and fete - August (third week). 'Blessing of the Sea' - Aug. E/C Th. Eating Out: Elements, Marine Drive. www.bude.co.uk or www.visitbude.info   also see www.budewebcam.co.uk

Bude Surfers at Sunset

Falmouth. This is one town where it is best to arrive by sea (like Venice) to fully appreciate its position, for it overlooks a superb natural harbour. You will then avoid the inevitable bottle-neck of traffic when you come to leave. If you do arrive by car, park by the harbour and walk up the narrow high street brimming with independents; galleries, organic foodies, tea rooms. The new university at Tremough Campus has brought youthful exuberance to the town, and brisk business. The Phoenicians and Romans came here in search of tin, and in the late C16, Sir Walter Raleigh persuaded the Killigrew family to develop the harbour's potential, and for 200 years it became the centre of the Mail Packet Trade, smuggling and piracy. Today, it is a popular yachting centre and home to these cultural venues: Pendennis Castle*, Maritime Museum*, Art Gallery*, gardens*, cinema, 3-beaches. Regatta week - mid Aug. E/C W. Eating Out: The Wheel House, Upton Slip, 01326 318050. The Provedore Tapas Bar & Cafe, 43 Trelawney Rd., 01326 314888, Harbour Lights fishn'chips, Arwenack St., 01326 316934. Gylly Café, Gyllngvase Beach, Cliff Rd., 01326 312884, or for an expensive treat: Indaba Fish, Swanpool Beach, 01326 311886.

Fowey. Pronounced Foy. Fowey is a chic and fashionable town of narrow streets and brightly coloured houses that overlooks another superb, natural harbour. A haven for yachtsmen, and a commercial seaport, and, an attractive option with many pubs, delis, restaurants, galleries and shops. Look out Padstow you have some serious competition! This was one of England's busiest towns in the Middle Ages, and home of the 'Fowey Gallants', a bunch of reckless and invincible pirates who raided French and Spanish shipping. Today, still a busy exporter of China Clay, for you may witness the large ships delivering their cargo to which appears out-of-sync in this holiday town. The Daphne Du Maurier Literary Centre (TIC) holds an annual festival. Museum*, Aquarium*, Fishing trips and passenger ferry to Polruan. Royal Regatta & Carnival week - Aug (2/3 week). Eating Out: Sam's, Fore St., 01726 832273. www.samsfowey.co.uk The Bistro, 24 Fore St., 01726832322.

Truro College
Fistral Beach

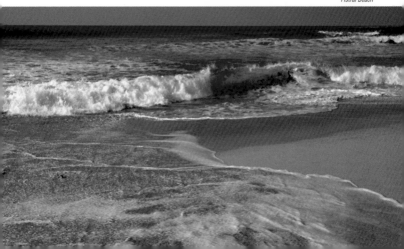

Padstow Harbour

Helston. The market town for the Lizard Pensinsula and venue for the Floral Dance held around the 8th May. Elegantly dressed couples dance through the streets to welcome the coming of Spring. The locals take the opportunity to sample unusual quantities of the Spingo brew in the Blue Anchor, and often miss their step on leaving. Beware of the open drains. Don't miss the sophisticated Georgian houses in Church and Coineagehall Street. Birthplace of Henry Trengrouse, inventor of the rocket lifesaving signals. Boating lake, CAST Studios*, Folk Museum*, Flambards *. Harvest Fair - Sept (Ist week). Eating out: Potager Garden & Glasshouse Cafe, Constantine, F & W/Es 10-5. 01326 341258.

Newquay. We all have our opinions of Newquay, and whatever they are, you can not argue with the superb beaches that have established Newquay as Cornwall's foremost surfing centre, and destination for partying youth, where it gets its fair share of hen, and stag parties, and thus suffers the blight of many English towns for the unruly and anti-social behaviour. For all of that, billions of pounds of property development has, and is, taking place. Tacky, old hotels and guest houses are being pulled down and are making way for luxurious apartments, evident as you head towards Fistral. To the north and south, outside of the town, are the quieter beaches. It, thus has, all the facilities of a modern resort; indoor and outdoor pools, Zoo*, Blue Reef Aquarium*. Fishing/boat trips from Quay, and a proliferation of camp sites. Carnival week - end May/early June. Eating Out: The Boathouse, South Quay Hill, 01637 874062.

Padstow. A labyrinth of narrow alleyways, and picturesque houses, and a safe haven on the treacherous North Coast. May Day heralds the arrival of the Padstow Hobby Horse ('Obby 'Oss) who prances and dances the streets taunting young, and not so young, maidens. A celebration of spring fever, and the coming of summer. C16 Raleigh's Court House on South Quay. C15 church. Boat trips. Centre of fine cuisine with many restaurants, most notably Rick Stein's various enterprises. Some have labeled the town, Padstein. A little unfair. True, he may have dominated our TV screens for an Age, but his success has rippled out across Cornwall, and made this old county a destination for lovers of seafood and local produce. It is worth walking away from the crowded harbour, and exploring the side streets, or heading out for the coastal footpath to the nearby beaches. The Camel Trail starts here, and you can hire a bike from one of the hirers located beside the car park at the bottom of the hill. Eating Out: Stein's Café, Deli and fishn'chips, or Bin Two, South Quay, Jacks at Parnalls Court or Rojanos, Mill Square. Spoilt for choice? www.padstow-cornwall.co.uk or www.padstow.com

Falmouth Harbour >

Penzance. A lively and busy town tempered by a lovely climate, for sub-tropical flowers grow in the Morrab Gardens and, at nearby, Trengwainton*. The Town Trail takes you to Chapel Street (where you will find exquisite shops, galleries and restaurants), and the Egyptian House*, and to Market Jew Street, dominated by the Ionic columns of Market House, and the Statue of Sir Humphrey Davy, inventor of the miners' Davy lamp. Look out for the Floating Harbour, and the ship Scillonia, which will ferry you to the Isles of Scilly, and besides you can also book shark and deep sea fishing trips. Other attractions; the swimming pools (in & outdoor), Penlee House Museum*. West Cornwall Spring Show - late March. Eating out: The Honeypot, Parade St., Sophia's Café, The Promenade and The Navy Inn, Queen Street.

St Ives. A labyrinth of narrow streets, whitewashed cottages, brightly coloured boats and sandy beaches so bright, piercing and clear, you could be forgiven you believed you had arrived in a Mediterranean village. The light drew in the early painters in the C19 and C20, and the sea has a magical turquoise colour, and today very much the southwest's centre for contemporary arts and crafts. Also, a centre for fine cuisine, especially locally-caught seafood. Its charm remains unaltered by the thousands who flock here. It is a special place worth exploring and, you never know, you may benefit from one of the art courses on offer. Barbara Hepworth Museum*, Leach Pottery*, Tate St Ives*. Music & Arts Festival - Sept. Eating out: Tate St Ives Coffee Shop, or The Loft, Norway Lane, Seafood Café, 45 Fore St., and The Wave, St Andrews St.

Truro. This is Cornwall's Cathedral city, administrative centre, and the major shopping centre in the county, always a hustle and bustle. There are elegant and beautiful buildings of the Georgian and Regency period, and on Lemon Street, the Assembly Rooms of 1772, the Mansion House and Prince's House in Princes Street, and the Cathedral*, 1880-1910. The City has seen much deveolpment of late; there are multiple stores and offices, and flats overlooking the river, and a wealth of contemporary architecture at Truro College, and with the new hospital buildings. Art Gallery & Museum*. Cinema. Eating out: Hub Burger Box, Lemon Quay, Charlotte's Tea House, Boscawen St., Restaurant Gaudi, 8 Edward St., and Idaba Fish, Tabernacle St.

The Harbour, St Ives

Penzance Docks

St Michael's Mount ss

SMALLER CENTRES

Camborne & Redruth. These two towns appear as one. Formerly Cornwall's great mining centre, and the hive of great endeavor, industry and skill. The birthplace of Richard Trevithick, 1771 - 1833 designer of the high-pressure steam pump which revolutionized mining, enabling water to be pumped out at great depths. Tin mining halted in the 1930s due to imports of cheap Malaysian tin. There are some handsome buildings to be seen and many pretty rows of terraced houses, which if up country, would be in great demand. Cinema. www.camborneonline.co.uk

Cawsand & Kingsand. Twin villages with narrow streets and colourful houses. Former C18 smuggling centre, and anchorage for Plymouth. Park in Kingsand and walk through to Cawsand, the prettier of the two, and stroll across to the ancient pilchard works. Plenty of pubs to savour – you may have found your true home? Fine walks along the coast to Cremyll Ferry. Eating out: Morans Café (B&B), 01752 829257.

Hayle. Formerly a small port and industrial centre. The foundries once made all the castings for every Cornish mine, and at nearby Copperhouse there were tin and copper smelting works. The 'Saltings' is a reserve for migratory birds. 3 miles of superb sand and Paradise Park*.

Marazion. Reputed to be the oldest town in Cornwall. Lies opposite St Michaels Mount* and thus the embarkation point for thousands who rarely venture into this village. The safe sandy beach, and children's playground are an added family attraction. Reputedly, Joseph of Arimathea traded here in tin. Classical galleried Methodist chapel built in 1862. Many art galleries. Eating out: Delicious Deli & Café, Fore St. 01736 711879, Ben's Cornish Kitchen, West End, 01736 719200

Lostwithiel. A charming town, and a great favourite of mine, often overlooked because travellers fail to drive off the main road into the side streets. The C13 capital of Cornwall, and as the Stannary capital oversaw the administration of the medieval tin industry. Hence, the wonderful mix of architecture - the town is packed with beautiful buildings: C13 Duchy Palace on Quay Street, C13 Parish Church, C17 and C18 Georgian houses on Fore Street and C18 Guildhall. Not forgetting, the C13 bridge, and all is set amidst the beautiful Fowey Valley . Outside the town, up a steep hill, Restormel Castle*. May Making ceremony, 'Beating the Hounds' - May (1st Monday) Gala week - late July. Festival week - end of August. Regatta -Aug BH. E/C W. Eating out: Trewithen Restaurant, Fore St. 01208 872373, Globe Inn, 01208 872501 and Duchy Coffee/ Tea shop, Fore St.

St Agnes. A former mining community, hence the skyline is jagged with disused engine houses. There is an arty ambience to this corner of Cornwall, quite different from other parts, perhaps more akin to Penwith. The birthplace of John Opie in 1761, Cornwall's most famous painter who became a Fellow of the Royal Academy at 26 and who is buried in St Paul's Cathedral. Family resort and centre for dramatic coastal walks. Museum. Arts & Crafts Trail. This is one of my favourite areas in Cornwall. HQ of "Surfers Against Sewage". Eateries: St Agnes Hotel, Churchtown, 01872 552307, Driftwood Spars Hotel, 01872 552428 and Schooners Bistro, 01872 553149 both in Trevaunance Cove. www.stagnes.info or www.st-agnes.com or www.sas.org.uk

St Austell. The proximity of first Heligan, and then Eden, has brought unheralded attention to this old brewing and route centre, whose original prosperity came from the china clay industry. The hinterland is made up of white mountainous pyramids, man-made lakes and palm trees. All heady stuff. Within the town, the fine C15 perpendicular church, the Holy Trinity, the C18 coaching inn, the White Hart and a Georgian Quaker House of 1829, all toll for the town's historic fortunes. To savour the adventures of the town's former merchants make your way to Charlestown, and admire the tall ships in dock.

St Germans. This was Cornwall's Cathedral City until 1043, and you are in no doubt of this when you stand before the superb Norman doorway to the church of St Germanus*. Next door, Port Eliot, was for centuries the seat of the Eliot family who now hold the annual Literary and Music Festival. The St Germans or Lynher River estuary is one of the great natural secrets of Cornwall. Elephant Fayre - July (last W/E). www.porteliot.co.uk

Wheal Coates

Old Pichard Works, Cawsand

St Just-in-Penwith. A handsome little town, formerly a hectic mining centre with an imposing Doric-facaded Methodist church. The area is rich in prehistoric antiquities, and rich in artists and craftsman (and many galleries*). By Bank Square, the amphitheatre 'Plain-an-Gwary'. Water sports festival, Priest's Cove – July. Eating out: The Cookbook, Cape Cornwall St. 01736 787266.

Tintagel. The village is composed of a long, and rather uninspiring high street, peopled with tacky gift shops and tearooms, which originally existed to service the pilgrims and visitors to Tintagel Castle. The setting is spectacular and strange and it is easy to fantasize about Merlin, and magic. For remarkable views, and a sense of Nature's violence, take a walk onto the Island and around the Castle, then out to the neighbouring outcrops: Barras Nose and Willapark, particularly spectacular on a stormy day. This is the perfect place to immerse yourself in Arthurian legend, as inspired by Geoffrey of Monmouth in the C12, and later by Tennyson's 'The Idylls of the King'. Summer Carnival. Visitor Centre. Eating out: The Olive Garden, Atlantic Rd., 01840 779270. www.tintagelweb.co.uk

You May Also Like to Consider..

Wadebridge. A busy and feel-good market town that has seen much recent development; new shops, eateries and galleries have brought a buzz and liveliness to this old, sleepy town, and venue for the Royal Cornwall Show in June. Magnificent C15 bridge with 17 arches. Superb views from the New Bridge on the A39. Mid-point for cycling the Camel Trail. Cinema. E/C W. Eating out: Relish, Foundry Court, 01208 814214, Raj Bar, Eddystone Place, 01208 895453 and The Dancing Taipan, The Platt, 01208 816623. www.visitwadebridge.com or www.royalcornwallshow.org

Mousehole

HARBOURS

Boscastle. An Attractive village within a steep valley leads down to a sinuous and dramatic harbour. A safe haven on a treacherous coastline, and despite this, it remains an extremely difficult portal destination to navigate into (especially on a stormy night). More recently, featured in the national news following the horrific flooding on the 16th August 2004. Cars and caravans were swept into the sea. Houses and shops were destroyed. The Royal Naval helicopter squadron from Chivenor, North Devon was magnificent in their efforts to save life, and limb. There are two cafés down by the harbour.
www.boscastlecornwall.org.uk
www.visitboscastleandtintagel.com

Cadgwith. Thatched cottages of green serpentine rock, boats beached on the shingle cove create a romantic scene. Haunt of artists. Superb coastal scenery. Eating out: Cafe. Inn.

Charlestown. There's a nostalgic atmosphere about this C18 port built by Charles Rashleigh. Still a busy exporter of china clay. Shipwreck and Heritage Museum*, Diving centre. Pottery. Often used as a location for TV/Films; Onedin Line, Longitude, Poldark, Rebecca and Rosemary Pilcher's novels. Eating out: The Harbourside Inn, Charlie's Coffee House.

Mevagissey. One of Cornwall's most picturesque and unspoilt fishing villages. The fine inner, and more recent outer, Harbour have been at the centre of the town's history. The Phoenicians and Romans traded here. Shark fishing centre, World of Model Railways*, Galleries*, Folk Museum* and Feast of St Peter - June (last week). Eating out: Country Kitchen, St Georges Square and The Alvorado, Polkirt Hill, or The School House, Pentewan.

Mousehole. Pronounced 'Mouzel'. The least spoilt of all Cornish fishing villages, and the author's favourite. Stone cottages huddle around the harbour facing east, sheltered from the prevailing winds. Wander the streets and discover art galleries and special eateries, and if in need of a rest, sit on the harbour wall and watch a time capsule of Cornish life pass you by. Originally called Port Enys when it was sacked, and burnt down by Spanish privateers in 1595. More recently, memories still linger of the terrible tragedy that struck the village in December 1981 when the Penlee Lifeboat, the Solomon Browne, and its 8-man crew perished in appalling weather. Fishing trips, carnival - Aug (2nd/3rd week). Galleries*. Eating out: Cornish Range, Chapel St., 2 Fore St., snd the Ship Inn.

Newlyn. Home of Cornwall's largest fishing fleet, and at day break, the lively fish market is in full voice. The medieval quay is a delight. Like St Ives, a favourite haunt for artists - Edwardian painters came, and left much work behind. Sadly, much of Newlyn was destroyed by Spanish Raiders in 1595, and by the Penzance Council in 1937 when 85% of the fisherman's cottages were pulled down. Art Gallery*. Fresh fish and shell fish merchants, aplenty. The pubs tend to be patronised by thirsty trawlermen. If you can cope with that you may experience something new. Eating out: Tolcarne Inn. www.tolcarneinn.co.uk

Penryn. An attractive town with a picturesque steep main street and handsome Georgian houses is situated at the head of Penryn Creek. Granted a Charter in 1236, and thus a much older community than nearby, Falmouth. In the C17, England's busiest port after London. In the C19, the export of granite began, and has continued supplying New Scotland Yard, four London Bridges and the Fastnet Lighthouse. The home of the Tremough Campus, the new University and Art College buildings of the University of Falmouth (& Exeter). Museum*. Town Fair - Aug BH W/E. Eating Out: Miss Peapod's Kitchen Café, Jubilee Wharf, 01326 374424. www.misspeapod.co.uk

Newlyn

Polperro

Polperro. The quintessential and "Pretty As A Picture" idyll of a Cornish fishing village. It is, yes, picturesque; for indeed, a timeless ambience pervades the narrow streets, pastel-shaded cottages and colourful harbour. It can be crowded during the day. Best visited in the evening when most are dining. And, you can enjoy a pint at the Blue Peter Inn, and if in luck, listen to the Fisherman's Choir practicing. Model Village and tea/gift shops. Fishing trips and Regatta; mid-July.

Port Isaac. A charming little port; a steep street runs down to a little harbour, hazardous when a northerly wind blows. Lobster fishing centre. Trips for mackerel, pleasant inns and parking (charge) on beach at I.T. Pottery. Fresh fish merchant. Location for the TV serial, Doc Martin, and the film Saving Grace. St Endellion Music Festival - Aug. Eating out on the Harbour Front: The Slipway Hotel, 01208 880264 and The Mote Bar, 01208 880226.

Porthleven. Attractive harbour with shipbuilding yard, C19 Harbour House and imposing Wesleyan chapel c.1890. The vulnerable harbour faces south west and was built for the mining industry in 1811. A south-westerly gale in 1824 washed it away, to be later rebuilt in 1855, with lock gates. Serious surf reef off the Harbour wall. Eating out: Amelies at The Smoke House.

Port Isaac

You May Also Like to Consider:

Looe. You may think you are in a time-warp, Looe is still an active, and scruffy, Cornish fishing village with a bustling quay, tidal harbour and a web of narrow streets that provides an unforgettable tableaux of Cornish life. And, you are better for the experience. It still has the cheap gift shops, and smell of chip batter. But, you can buy fresh fish collected off the boats that morning, or you can walk the Looe Valley Line where a number of way-marked trails lead off along 8-miles of railway track from Looe to Liskeard. It's an embarkation point for deep-sea fishing trips. Fish market on East Looe Quay. Sub-Aqua Club. Eating Out: Top end nosh: Trawlers Restaurant on The Quay: 01503 263593, alternatively: Sarah's Pasty Shop, Buller Street, 01503 263973.

Porthleven

VILLAGES OF INTEREST

St Mawes

Altarnun. A bit off the beaten track, but when all is said, it is a charming linear village with a superb C16 church*, the 'Cathedral of the Moors', and worthy of your attention. Packhorse bridge. Inn.

Calstock. A sprawling, former river port on the river Tamar. The thickly wooded river bank has an abundance of fruit growing, and provides splendid colour in Spring. The 12-arch viaduct is a memorable sight, too. Numerous disused mining chimneys and engine houses continue to haunt the landscape.

Coverack. A charming, picturesque old fishing village and former smuggling centre given to bucket and spade holidays. Small harbour.

Lamorna. A pretty village beside a wooded valley, and since the Newlyn School, a favourite of artists and craftsmen. Summer craft exhibitions. Small jetty, and cafe at cove. Inn.

Morwenstow. Famous for Richard Stephen Hawker (1803-75); the eccentric and original vicar-poet, and originator of harvest festivals. A compassionate man, he would stalk the wild coast in beaver hat, fisherman's long boots and yellow cloak in search of shipwrecked sailors. Many are buried in his churchyard. And, to stir (or wake) his congregation he would often dress up as a mermaid. Rectory Tearooms, opposite the church. Bush Inn.

Mullion. A busy village, and centre for much of the Lizard Peninsula. There is a splendid church, some popular pubs and cafes, an active cricket club, and an award-winning school. The one-way system will draw you in, and dismiss you, but first bear left, and make your way down to the Cove. The beaches close to: Poldhu and Polurrian are often empty but for a local dog walker. Eating out: Mullion Cove Bistro, Polurrian Cove Hotel.

Polruan. An attractive village with a busy boatyard. The main street plunges almost vertically to the small quay. Cars not encouraged. Superb views from the hill top car park. Worth the excitement of taking the pedestrian ferry to and from, Fowey. The coastal walks are quite flat and re-assuring. Lugger Inn.

Port Quin. A little hamlet with a few rental cottages, pebble beach and the C19 folly, Doyden Castle used as the home of Dr Dwight Enys in the Poldark TV series. Invigorating clifftop walks.

St Mawes. This village is staid and middle class, and full of second-homes. It is thus popular with yachties, and their groupies. It is the main centre for the beautiful Roseland Peninsula and home to the Forte Family's, Hotel Tresanton, set in an enviable position and worthy of your purse's attention. Castle.

Saltash. Most will rush past this little port and forget about it. An inspection of I K Brunel's bridge may be the exception to your rule, and you will be rewarded with chains of parabolas. The steep streets descend to the Tamar estuary. May Fair – 1st week. Regatta – June 3rd week.

Sennen Cove. This isolated and independent community have for years made a precarious living from the sea. The old Lifeboat Station, proud of a heroic history was established in 1853. The stone pier in 1905. Whitewashed cottages, and the Round House Gallery* line the front. It is popular surfing centre. Look out for the Celtic Cross in the car park. A visit to this shrine may improve your turns and barrels. Fishing trips. Café. Inn.

Sennen Cove

Porthmeor Beach, St Ives

Cornwall is perhaps best known for its coastline and the multitude of beaches that pepper it. Nowhere in England is there such a quantity and variety of beaches – from wide, flat and open windswept beaches akin to many in the Southern Hemisphere, to tiny rocky coves with caves and imposing cliffs. Whether you want a safe place to visit with your family, somewhere to paddle in the shallows and eat ice cream, or if you want the rawness of nature to take your breath away, there are plenty of choices.

Bedruthan Steps, Nr Newquay.
One of Cornwall's most dramatic beaches with a series of rock stacks crossing it which legend says were built by a giant named Bedruthan, who used them as stepping stones to traverse the bay. If you can negotiate the access which is via a very steep slippery staircase, you reach firm golden sands with massive rocks and caves.

Daymer Bay, Nr Rock.
Popular family beach – ideal for young children due to its firm golden sands and sheltered position.

Fistral, Newquay.
This is the most popular surf beach in Cornwall and the clarity of the turquoise water is unparalleled. There are wide sands even at high tide and cafés for snacks to sustain you while you people watch.

Kynance Cove, Nr Lizard.
At low tide, there are white sands and good bathing (in summer) as well as serpentine rocks shaped over centuries by the rushing tides. At high tide it is too dangerous to swim but you can listen to the roaring noise of blow-holes and watch the violence of nature up close and personal. Get there early at low tide in summer and you could believe you were on a desert island.

Porthcurno, Nr Sennen.
This is a white shell sand beach washed by turquoise sea and surrounded by high granite cliffs - a place of real beauty.

Watergate Bay

Bedruthan Steps

Porthleven Sands, Gunwalloe

Daymer Bay

Porthleven Sands, Nr Helston. The steep shelving beach has a strong undertow and swimming is not encouraged making it less suitable for families. Ideal for a brisk walk across the four miles of sands – blowing away the cobwebs and enjoying the fantastic views across to Mounts Bay.

Porthmeor, St Ives. Just one of St Ives fabulous town beaches which is well served by local eateries and overlooked by the Tate St Ives. Wide flat sands at low tide and popular with all.

Sandy Mouth, Nr Kilkhampton. Expansive beach with swift currents and strong rip tides making it popular with surfers. Fabulous rock formations that glow at dusk. Firm sands and rock pools at low tide.

Trebarwith Strand, Nr Tintagel. Extraordinary rock formations at the head of the beach. Very attractive at dusk when the setting sun hits the surrounding cliffs.

Watergate Bay, Nr Newquay. One of the few beaches in Cornwall that you can see from the road. It affords fantastic vistas even when you're just driving by. Very popular for extreme sports, therefore good for people watching.

White Beach, Porthcurno

Widemouth Sands

Marsland Mouth to Bude: Approx. 19 miles. A remote and wild coastline; the rocks, razor sharp and contorted, the pathway hard going, yet exhilarating and rewarding. Rest at Morwenstow* and visit the church* and tearoom or Inn. Onwards, passing Parson Hawker's Hut and two miles on, the white satellite dish aerials of GCHQ at Cleave Camp, then into Duckpool where a path leads up to the Coombe Valley Nature Trail*. At low tide one can follow the sands to Bude, or take the cliff top path.

Bude to Boscastle Harbour: Approx. 15 miles. Up to Compass Point for extensive views northwards. The path overlooks reefs, buttresses and pinnacles. Easy going to Widemouth Sands. Through car park, up Penhalt Cliff to Millook Haven with cliffs of contorted slate. Rough ascent to Dizzard Point (500ft), prone to landsliding, then onto veined and contorted rock forms of Pencannow Point. Easy

Trebarwith Strand

Treyarnon Bay

descent to the fine sands of Crackington Haven, cafe. Hard going up to Cambeak - views from Hartland Point to Trevose Head. Climbing beside further landslipped sections, to pass jagged cliffs and The Strangles (beach), scene of many shipwrecks, to High Cliff, at 731ft the highest cliff in Cornwall (although slumping has created a massive sloping undercliff so it lacks the drama of a precipice) and supposedly a favourite courting and riding spot for Thomas Hardy and his first wife, Emma Gifford. Then, to Beeny Cliff, the only headland carved from Chert, a tough black flint-like rock, and often below, basking seals. Along to Pentaragon Waterfall which falls 100ft down a deep chasm. And, the respite of Boscastle Harbour* for refreshments, via Penally Point, and the tortuous harbour entrance.

Boscastle Harbour to Port Isaac: Approx. 12 miles. The cliff walk to Tintagel along springy turf with spectacular views seaward to jagged rocks, is quite superb. Worth a diversion inland, to visit Rocky Valley, and St Nectan's Kieve*, tearoom, a 40ft waterfall, and ancient hermitage. Returning to the coast path; offshore Lye Rock, once a renowned puffin colony - now the cliffs are nesting sites for fulmars, guillemots, razorbills and shags. The landscape is wild and remote, a place of legend, and the romantic setting for the C13 Tintagel Castle* and the mass of older remains on Tintagel Island. On leaving the castle ruins, the path climbs sharply to the cliff top church of St Materiana, guardian of many shipwrecked sailors. Along Glebe Cliff past numerous old slate quarries to Trebarwith Strand*,café, a lovely beach to freshen up before the switchback path to Port Isaac*.

Padstow to Newquay: Approx. 16 miles. A coastline dotted with superb sandy beaches and pounded by the mighty Atlantic rollers, but best appreciated out of season. Splendid views at Stepper Point, then on past caves and sheer cliffs at Butter Hole and Pepper Hole. The path hugs the coastline passing by campsites and beaches ideal for a quick dip. Look out for the emerald waters of Mother Ivey. The coastline is peppered with stacks and islands; none more spectacular than at Bedruthan Steps*, NT café, where legend has it that these stacks were used as stepping stones by the Cornish giant, Bedruthan. Walk the clifftops in summer and bathe in the carpets of wild flowers that fill the air with the scent of burnet rose and gorse. Reaching Stem Point, it's possible to walk the sands to Newquay at low tide; alternatively the headland path is easy going.

Entrance to Boscastle Harbour

St Ives to Land's End: Approx. 22 miles. Considered to be the finest stretch of all: wild, rugged and besieged, relentlessly, by the elements. The path is lonely and remote, up and down, up and down, and at times, hard going, as it follows the cliff edge, and clifftop. Seals laze on the Carracks. A blow hole roars below Zennor Head. It's worth a detour to Zennor for refreshments and to meet the Mermaid in the church. On to Gurnard's Head (great pub), sphinx-like with great views, and now you are entering the heart of tin mining country, so beware of unprotected mine shafts. The cliffs between St Ives and Pendeen may glitter with minerals. Hereabouts, paths criss-cross in all directions, and there's much to interest the industrial archaeologist, especially at Geevor, Levant and Botallack. Following the clifftops, Cape Cornwall appears, marked by a lonely stack, the remains of a mine abandoned in the 1870s. The cliff drops to

High Tide, Bedruthan Steps

Evening Light, Land's End

every cranny and contour, the second cuts off along the headlands for a wonderfully invigorating walk. Down into tiny Porthgwarra, and on up to St Levan's Well above the little cove of Porthchapel. Then along to Porthcurno passing the famous Minack Theatre*; below, an improbably turquoise sea, and the outline of Logan's Rock. On you must walk around the dramatic granite columns of Treen Cliff, and then by Cribba Head, to the tiny fishing cove of Penberth. Along clifftops to Lamorna Cove, café, a favourite spot for artists. The path continues along the clifftop until Mousehole*.

Porthleven to Lizard: Approx. 13 miles. Interesting coastal path; craggy cliffs and splendid sandy beaches. The path follows cliff edge to Loe Bar*, Gunwalloe and Church Cove; apparently buried treasure is hidden here. Onto the caves, arches and black rocks of Mullion Cove. Fine walking on clifftops around Vellan Head, and past breathtaking precipices, to Pigeon Ogo, a vast amphitheatre of rock. The crowning glory is Kynance Cove, a spectacle of swirling currents (at HT), whooshing blow holes and wild-shaped serpentine rocks, great bathing at LT, and a great cafe. Then on along the well-trod path to Britain's most southerly point, Lizard Point. Caves and caverns about Polpeor Cove. East is the Lion's Den, a large collapsed sea-cave, a sudden vast hole in the cliff turf. Café.

Godrevy Island Lighthouse

Aire Point, and ahead lies the thunderous breakers, and dedicated surfers, of Whitesand Bay. Café. And, now the well worn path to Land's End. This is a sad case of where commercialism has ruined the natural landscape. It is obvious that if you look around at the appalling state of the footpaths you will surmise that the caretakers of this promontory have little regard for its future. As the old proverb puts it: "We do not inherit the earth from our ancestors, we borrow it from our children", or as Henry Ford so gallantly explained: "A business that makes nothing but money is a poor business." From the coastal footpath the natural landscape is indeed a sight to behold. There are dramatic cliffs and rock falls, and when the light is exacting the sunsets can be magnificent.

Land's End to Mousehole: Approx. 15 miles. Yet, another superb stretch of coastline; precipitous cliffs, great blocks of granite, sandy coves and minute valleys with sub-tropical vegetation. Spectacular rock formations to Gwennap Head, equally as wild a headland as Land's End. Here are great, gnarled, granite boulders, cracked and sculpted by the elements; a popular place for climbers, and below, a haunt for seals. There are two paths: the first follows

Kynance Cove

Lizard to Falmouth: Approx. 26 miles. The east side of the peninsula is less rugged, the slopes are gentler, the landscape becomes more hospitable as one travels northward. First, you pass pretty Church Cove, and along the clifftop to the Devil's Frying Pan, a larger version of the Lion's Den that roars when the easterlies blow. Through thatched Cadgwith, to Kennack Sands, where the path is easy-going, hugging the cliff edge, and almost at sea level from Coverack to Lowland Point, scene of an Ice Age 'Raised Beach'. Offshore, at low tide 'The Manacles' are visible, a treacherous reef that has caused the death of more than 400 drowned sailors, many lie buried (and forgotten) in St Keverne's churchyard. The 60ft spire of the church serves as a daymark for sailors and fishermen. At Godrevy Cove, the path turns inland to Rosenithon and Porthoustock to avoid quarries, returning to the coast at Porthallow. A peaceful stretch to Gillan Harbour, possible to wade the creek at low tide, or continue to bridge crossing the head of the creek at Carne. Through tangled woods to Helford village and ferry across Helford estuary, which runs from Easter to end of October, to either Helford Passage or the beach at Durgan. From here the path passes Mawnan Church and along the clifftops to Falmouth.

Par Sands to Looe: Approx. 18 miles. Lovely walk through pretty Polkerris, café, then up to the impressive cliffs of Gribbin Head (224ft) and an 84ft landmark erected by Trinity House in the 1820s. Fine views from the Lizard to Rame Head. At Polridmouth, sub-tropical flora and on up the path with good views of Fowey Harbour. Passing near the remains of St Catherine's Castle. Follow the road into Fowey where there is a regular ferry to Polruan. Then six miles of magnificent lonely clifftop walking to Polperro. Inland grazed fields and gentler contours, but the coast path is steep and hard-going. Polperro* must be explored, then along a well maintained path following the cliff edge to Looe.

Looe to Cremyll: Approx. 21 miles. Soon to leave Cornwall's rugged coastline; Battern Cliffs (450ft), the highest cliffs in South Cornwall, remind one of the dramas left behind. Past the little harbour of Portwrinkle, the path hugs the cliff edge and you can now walk through the M.O.D. ranges at Tregantle, except during firing when you will be re-routed, inland. Around the great sweep of Whitsand Bay to Rame Head with views of Plymouth Sound beyond. Along to the twin villages of Kingsand and Cawsand, passing Mount Edgcumbe, and to Cremyll Ferry which has carried passengers across the Tamar since the C13. And, now for a pint, or two, of ale – or, maybe a foot massage? You deserve it!

Camel Estuary

Ogo-Dour, Lizard

Cycling Couple, Camel Trail

Bugle to the Eden Project, Nr St Austell.
6km/4miles, Crosses the heathlands of Treskilling Downs, past woodland and lakes.

Camel Trail (NCN 3 & 32), Padstow.
27km/17miles, Cornwall's most popular trail with an estimated 500,000 annual visitors. Bodmin to Padstow with deviation north to Poley's Bridge; also suitable for jogging, walking and bird watching. Cycle hire in Padstow and Wadebridge. Info on: 01872 327310.

Cardinham Woods, Nr Bodmin. 5km/3m circuit around woodland owned by the Forestry Commission. Also, 4-waymarked walks of 3-7.5km. Parking available. Café.

Coast to Coast Trail, Nr Truro. 17km/11miles, Park at the Bike Chain Bissoe Bike Hire. Connects two historic harbours, Portreath and Devoran, and passes by wildlife and ancient woodland.

Great Flat Lode Trail, Nr Redruth.
12km/7miles, Park at the Mineral Tramway Centre. A circular route exploring the landscape of tin and copper mines from the 1860s.

Pentewan Trail, Nr St Austell. 6km/4miles, An easy off-road route from London Apprentice to Pentewan with an off-shoot to Heligan Gardens that uses ½ mile of road. Bike hire.

Portreath Branchline Trail, Nr Redruth.
9km/5miles, Connects to the Great Flat Lode Trail by using quiet roads.

Redruth & Chasewater Railway Trail.
12km/7miles, Park at Twelveheads. Based on the old railway lines. It is mostly off-road with some major roads to cross.

Tehidy Trail, Nr Redruth. 4km/2.5miles, Park in Portreath. Linear route using the tracks and trails through Tehidy Country Park.

Wheal Martyn to the Eden Project, Nr St Austell.
8km/5miles, Cycle through clay country, woodland and heathland with stunning views. Bike hire.

Sailing Boat, Camel Trail

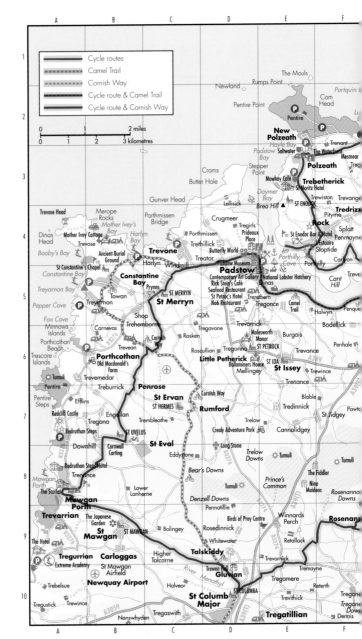

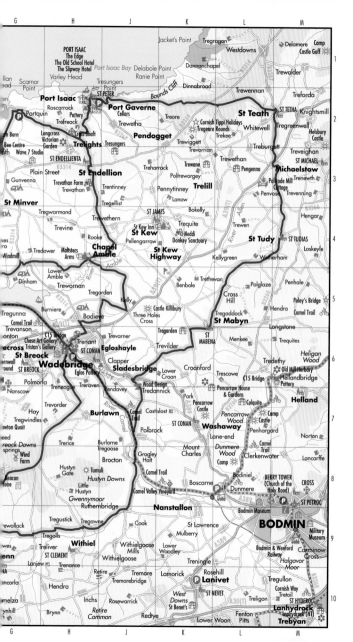

PREHISTORIC SITES

Chysauster Ancient Village, Nr Penzance. This is the best preserved Iron Age village in Cornwall, and with eight circular houses. It was occupied during the Roman Conquest. Strange that Cornwall has so few Roman remains. Access is via a half-mile long path from the road.

Hurlers Stone Circle, Minions. Three stone circles 110ft, 135ft and 105ft in diameter. According to legend - Men turned to stone for playing the old Cornish game of Hurling on a Sunday. It is a similar game to Australian Rules. Access is via a 1/4 mile path from road.

Lanyon Quoit (NT), Nr Madron. A Stone Age dolmen with 3-uprights, and a Capstone re-erected c.1824.

Men An Tol

The Cheesewring, Nr Minions. An extraordinary formation of granite slabs weathered by wind and rain. A Bronze Age cup (now residing in the British Museum) was found in a grave on Stowe's Hill.

Trethevy Quoit, Tremar. An impressive Neolithic dolmen. The 6-uprights support a massive Capstone, pierced by a circular hole.

Zennor Quoit. This is one of England's largest dolmens. A double-chambered tomb with massive slab. Pieces of Neolithic pottery discovered here.

Lanyon Quoit

Men-An-Tol, Nr Morvah. A large circular slab with a hole pierced through the centre is set between 2-upright slabs. Famous for its legendary magical healing powers - children were passed through to cure them of rickets (and insolence).

Merry Maidens Stone Circle, Nr Lamorna. These 19-stones form the perfect circle. Legend has it – of girls turned to stone for dancing on a Sunday.

Nine Maidens Stone Circle, Nr Morvah. 2-circles of standing stones, 50ft and 60ft in diameter.

Plain-An-Gwarry, St Just-In-Penwith. Circular embankment (cattle pen) where old Cornish miracle plays were performed.

Trevethy Quoit

The Cheesewring, Bodmin Moor >

Launcells Church

GREAT CHURCHES

Altarnun, St Nonna. Superb C16 church. The tall perpendicular tower rises to 109 ft. Norman font. C16 bench ends. Known locally as 'The Cathedral of the Moors'. Overlooks an attractive linear village.

Blisland, St Protus & St Hyacinth. Wonderfully restored church in village with attractive village green. C15 granite tower and Norman font. C15 brasses.

Bodmin, St Petroc. In the C6 Cornwall's patron saint, St Petroc founded a priory here. Later, in the C9 a monastery was established, and in the Middle Ages, the town became an important religious centre. The present church was mainly built in the C15. Norman font, Monuments and Wagon roof.

Launcells, St Swithins. Fortunate to be the only Cornish church not tampered with by the Victorians. Wall painting and 60 carved bench ends. Fabulous wagon roofs, note the carvings. All is situated in a divine valley.

Launceston, St Mary Magdalene. Noted for the famous exterior carved granite panels of foliage and shields that cover most of the walls. C14 tower, and a rare painted pulpit.

Morwenstow, St John the Baptist. Famous for the C19 poet-vicar, R S Hawker who buried many shipwrecked sailors in his churchyard. Impressive Norman doorway, wagon roof and wall paintings. In superb location overlooking the Atlantic Ocean.

St Germanus, St Germans. Founded as an Augustinian Priory, and later, a Cathedral in the Anglo-Saxon period. Only the South Aisle and Nave remain. Magnificent Norman doorway, and East Window glass by the pre-Raphaelite, Edward Burne-Jones.

St Neot. Imposing building in scenic valley famous for the 15 medieval stained glass windows. Perhaps, the finest glass in the West Country.

Tintagel, St Materiana. Of Norman origin, and Catholic empathy, this church defies erosive nature, and the storms she encounters in its isolated clifftop position. Visit on a dark, moody day, and be impressed.

Truro Cathedral. The first English Cathedral to be built since St Paul's. An imposing building, designed by John Pearson, in the Gothic style, 1880-1910. With three soaring spires, and an unrivalled collection of stained glass. Refectory for light meals, 10-4. Open M-Sa 7.30-6, Su 9-7. Shop and Chapter House from 10. www.trurocathedral.org.uk

St Neot

Truro Cathedral

CASTLES

Caerhays Castle & Gardens. 60 acres of informal woodland gardens created by J C Williams who had sponsored plant hunting expeditions to China. Noted for camellias, magnolias and rhododendrons. Garden open daily mid-Feb to early June, 10-5. Castle from mid-Mar 2-4 M-F & BHs. www.caerhays.co.uk

Caerhays Castle ss

Castle An Dinas, Nr Indian Queens. Four massive concentric rings; crowned by 'Roger's Tower', an C18 folly. Iron Age pottery found.

Fowey, St Catherine's Castle (EH). Few remains survive, of this former blockhouse built in 1536 to house a protective chain across the harbour mouth, in accord with Henry VIII's military policy. Viewpoint.

Launceston Castle (EH). Norman castle built in c.1070 with timber. It was the main seat of Robert de Mortain, brother of William the Conqueror. Rebuilt C12-13. Good example of a "motte and bailey" structure.

Pendennis Castle (EH), Falmouth. Built 1544-46 in the age of cannon and gunpowder, as one of a chain of castles Henry VIII erected from 1538 to deter French Invasion. Circular Keep with drawbridge, portcullis, spy holes and spiral staircase. Superb viewpoint. To the south east, the blockhouse built on the rocks.

Pengersick Castle. Fortified Tudor manor c. 1500 with evidence of an Apothecarian garden in the C14, to be renovated. "The most haunted house in the UK". With the death of the last owner, the late Angela Evans, the trustees have set forth to restore the castle with a grand opening planned. www.pengersickcastle.com

Restormel Castle (EH), Lostwithiel. A model of military architecture; classically symmetrical with circular moat, and strategically positioned allowing breathtaking views across the River Fowey. Built c.1100 with C13 additions. Owned by Simon de Montfort and Richard Earl of Cornwall.

St Mawes Castle (EH). Built in 1540-43 as a link in Henry VIII's chain of coastal defences. A fortress of striking symmetry; trefoil shaped with gun emplacements, drawbridge and heraldic decorations, and all set in sub-tropical gardens. Superb viewpoint.

St Michael's Mount (NT), Marazion. A legendary place of romance, and pilgrimage, and a child's dream of a fairy castle. Originally, the site of a Benedictine chapel established by Edward the Confessor. In the C14, the spectacular castle was added. Later, to be used as a nunnery, and military fortress, before the St Aubryn family purchased it in 1659, living here ever since. Church dates from 1275. Exquisite Blue Drawing Room with Chippendale furniture. Pictures by Gainsborough and the Cornish Artist, John Opie. Harbour, railway. 01736 710507. Open 26 Mar-2 Nov M-F & Su 10.30-5, Guided tours Nov-Mar if weather and tides permit. Mar-May Tu for pre-arranged educational visits. Church opens on Sunday at 10.30 for 11am Service. Restaurant and shop open daily Apr-Oct. Special family ticket available. Please Note: access on foot over the causeway at low tide, or during summer months only, by ferry at high tide (return ferry tickets should not be taken). Make sure the Mount is open before crossing on the ferry! www.stmichaelsmount.co.uk

Tintagel Castle (EH). An early Celtic settlement, 350-800 AD, later developed into this island fortress by the Earls of Cornwall in the C12 and C13s. Fragments of the Great Hall c.1250, the gate and walls survive. The wild and windswept coast, married with the romantic legends of King Arthur, and encouraged by Geoffrey of Monmouth and Tennyson's Idyll, (although doubted by scholars) provide an atmosphere of mystery and wonder.

Launceston Castle

HISTORIC BUILDINGS

Jamaica Inn, Bolventor. A former old coaching inn, and inspiration for Daphne du Maurier's novel. Bars, restaurants, accommodation & gift shops. Attractions include the Daphne du Maurier Room, 'The Smugglers at Jamaica Inn'. T 01566 86250. Inn open daily, all year.
www.jamaicainn.co.uk

Lizard Lighthouse. Large, famous building completed in 1752, with alterations in 1903. Stands amid treacherous coast, haunted by many shipwrecks. Renovated Engine Room. Climb the lighthouse tower. Visitor Centre open mid-March to Oct M-F, weather permitting.
www.trinityhouse.co.uk

Mount Edgcumbe House & Park. Sensitively restored Tudor mansion in beautiful landscaped parkland. Formal English, French and Italian Gardens. National Camellia Collection. T 01752 822236. Park and gardens open daily all year. House and Earl's Garden open Apr-Sept Su-Th 11-4.30.
www.mountedgcumbe.gov.uk

Great Hall, Prideaux Place ss

Pencarrow House. Georgian house set in extensive grounds. Fine collections of pictures, furniture and porcelain. Cafe, gift and plant shop, and children's play area. T 01208 841369. House open daily from Apr-Sept (gardens from 1 Mar-Oct 10-5) except F & Sa 11-5.
www.pencarrow.co.uk

Pendeen Lighthouse. Built in 1900 to protect vessels from Wra Rocks around Pendeen Watch. The lighthouse keeper's cottages are now let as holiday cottages and the automatic fog signal is controlled via a telemetry link from the Trinity House Operational Control Centre in Harwich.
www.trinityhouse.co.uk

Prideaux Place, Padstow. Home of the Prideaux-Brune family. Filled with treasures, pictures, portraits, porcelain and exquisite furniture. T 01841 532411. Open Easter week, then 9 May-7 Oct Su-Th 1.30-5. Grounds and tearoom from 12.30.
www.prideauxplace.co.uk

Mary Newman's Cottage, 48 Culver St., Saltash. C15 Cottage of Mary Newman, first wife of Sir Francis drake. Furniture supplied by the Victoria and Albert Museum. Open Apr-Nov W & Sa (July-Sept Th & F) from 10 (2 on W).
www.saltash.org.uk

King Arthur's Great Hall & Hall of Chivalry, Tintagel. A magnificent hall built in memory of King Arthur and his Knights, using 50 types of Cornish stone and 70 stained glass windows. The Arthurian Experience tells the story of Arthur and his Knights. Dogs welcome. T 01840 770526. Open daily; summer 10-5, winter 11-dusk.

Trelowarren, Nr Helston. Home of the Vyvyan family since 1427 and now a pioneering Eco-Timeshare development. Acres of woodland and farmland surround the house. Chateau camping, pottery, Cornish herbs and woodland walks. Cornwall Crafts Association shop. 15 self-catering cottages. New Yard Restaurant for late breakfasts, lunch and dinner. T 01326 222105. Garden open to customers 11-5 in season (no dogs).
www.trelowarren.co.uk

Wesley's Cottage, Trewint. John Wesley, the founder of Methodism, preached and rested during his preaching tours of Cornwall. Furnished in C18 style, collection of Wesleyana. Open summer Tu, F, Sa 10.30-3.30. 01566 782251
www.wesleycottage.org.uk

The Library, Antony House ss

NATIONAL TRUST PROPERTIES

Antony House & Gardens, Nr Torpoint. Built for Sir William Carew from 1711-1721, and considered the most distinguished example of early C18 architecture in Cornwall. Colonnades, panelled rooms and family portraits. Location for film "Alice In Wonderland". T 01752 812191. Open Easter to end Oct Tu, W, Th & BHMs 1.30-5.30 (also W/Es in June, July & Aug).

Cornish Mines & Engines, Nr Camborne. Cornwall's two great Beam Engines built in 1892 to pump out water from 550m, and for winding men and ore, up and down, the shaft. Restored to a pristine condition. Open mid-Mar to early Nov, M, W-F & SU, 11-5.

Cotehele House, Nr Calstock. Medieval house of grey granite built from 1485-1627 in a romantic position overlooking the River Tamar, and Devon, beyond. For centuries, the Edgcumbe family home, containing their original furniture, C17 tapestries, armour and needlework. The gardens lie on several levels. Medieval dovecote. Ancient clock in Chapel. Refreshments and shop. T 01579 351346. Open daily except F (house closed), mid-Mar to early Nov 11-5 (4.30 in Oct). Gardens open all year 10.30-dusk.

Glendurgan Gardens, Mawnan. Valley garden of great beauty with fine trees and shrubs, a maze, a giant's stride, a wooded valley of primulas and bluebells that runs down to Helford River. T 01326 252020. Garden open mid-Feb to end Oct Tu-Sa & BHMs 10.30-5.30.

Cotehele Quay ss

The White Room, Cotehele House ss

Taylor's Shaft, Cornish Engines, Camborne ss

Glendurgan Gardens ss >
Lanhydrock ss >

Godolphin House, Nr Helston. Romantic Tudor and Stuart Mansion, c.1475. The Godolphin family's courtly ambitions and taste are expressed in the evolving design of the house. Tin mining provided wealth for this family of entrepreneurs, soldiers, poets and officials. C16 and C17 English furniture. T 01736 763194. Garden open daily 10-4, House open as locally advertised. www.godolphinhouse.com

Lanhydrock House, Nr Bodmin. This is Cornwall's grandest house. C17, but largely rebuilt after the fire in 1881. Superb Victorian kitchens, magnificent plaster ceilings depicting scenes from the Old Testament, and a Long Gallery 116 feet long. C17 Gatehouse. Fine shrub and formal gardens. Woodland walks. Restaurants. Shop. T 01208 265950. Open daily Mar to early Nov except M when House only closed, but open BH Ms 11-5.30 (-5 in Oct), Nov-Mar Gardens open during daylight.

Levant Mine & Beam Engine, Pendeen. The oldest steam engine in Cornwall, restored after fifty years. Open all year F 10-5 (winter not steaming) plus East & Spring BHs, Su & M. June W Th F & Su. July-5 Oct Su-F 11-5, except M.

Tintagel, The Old Post Office. A miniature C14 manor house used in the C19 as a post office. Open daily mid-Mar to Oct 10.30-5.30 (4 in Oct).

Trelissick Garden, Nr Feock. Extensive park, farmland and woods. A large garden, lovely in all seasons, with beautiful views over the Fal Estuary and Falmouth Harbour. Woodland Walks beside River Fal. T 01872 862090. Open daily early Feb to end Oct 10.30-5.30 (sunset), winter daily 11-4. Shop and Art Gallery also open. Woodland walk open all year.

Trengwainton Garden, Nr Penzance. Large shrub garden with a vast collection of rhododendrons. Colourful in spring, and early summer. Views across Mounts Bay. T 01736 363148. Open mid-Feb to early Nov Su-Th 10.30-5.

You May Also Like To Consider:

Trerice, Nr Newquay. A delightful, small and secluded Elizabethan manor house rebuilt in 1571, containing magnificent fireplaces, plaster ceilings, oak and walnut furniture. Small lawn mower museum. Refreshments. Open daily mid-Feb to early Nov 11-5 (Gardens/shop from 10.30). www.nationaltrust.org.uk

The Eden Project

Antony Woodland Gardens. 100 acres of sprawling woodland, 103 magnolias, 300 types of camellias, and a plethora of azaleas, and rhododendrons, that border the River Lynher. Open Tu W Th & W/Es Mar-Oct 11-5.

Boconnoc. An ancient estate that can trace its history back to Norman times, and the Domesday Roll of 1087. A woodland, spring flowering garden, with a mass of hydrangeas and newly planted magnolias. Open every Sunday in May, and by appointment. T 01208 872507
www.boconnoc.com

Bosahan Garden, Manaccan. Lieing close to the Helford River, Bosagan has a micro-climate that encourages exotic palms, rhododendrons, azaleas and trees from southern climes. Open late Mar to mid-Sept M-F 10.30-4.30. T 01326 231351.

Bosvigo. A plantsman's garden, best seen in summer (June-Aug); with a series of enclosed and walled gardens and their herbaceous borders. Nursery. T 01872 275774. Open Mar-Sept W Th & F 11-6. www.bosvigo.com

Burncoose Nurseries & Gardens. 30 acre woodland garden. Also nursery with 3,000 varieties of trees, shrubs and unusual plants. Light refreshments. Owned by the Caerhays Estate. Open M-Sa 8.30-5 (Su 11-5). www.burncoose.co.uk

Carwinion Gardens. Valley garden with camellias, rhododenrons, azaleas, wild flowers and 100 species of bamboo. Incorporating Towan Camellia and Hydrangea Nursery. T 01326 250258. Open daily 10-5.30. B&B accommodation. www.carwinion.co.uk

Eden Project. The world-famous project that converted old china clay pits into vast steel-framed domes housing a tropical rain forest, and a Mediterranean climate. This project of great vision, and ambition, has drawn visitors in their hundreds of thousands since opening in Spring 2000. T 01726 811911. Open daily from 10. www.edenproject.com

The Lost Gardens of Heligan ss

Enys Gardens. The oldest garden in Cornwall, and the home of Robert de Enys who lived here during the reign of Edward 1. Bluebells galore! Open Apr-Sept Tu & Th 2-5, and the first Su of the month.
www.enystrust.org.uk

Lost Gardens of Heligan, The. With over 200 acres to explore, be sure to give yourself a full day to enjoy these stunning pleasure grounds; a Living Museum of C19 horticulture, and one of the most inspiring restoration projects in history. For its success gave rise to the Eden Project. T 01726 845100. Open daily 10-6 (winter -5).
www.heligan.com

Penjerrick Gardens. Described as a Jungle Garden. Yet, it is essentially a spring-flowering garden of 16 acres with an abundance of camellias, azaleas, rhododendrons and tree ferns. There are magnificent trees, pond gardens, bamboo and a woodland walk. T 01872 870105. Open Mar-Sept W, F & Su 1.30-4.30.
www.penjerrickgarden.co.uk

You May Also Like To Consider:

Trebah Gardens. Magical sub-tropical ravine gardens running down to private beach on Helford River, a canvas of ever-changing colour from Spring to Autumn. A garden for the plantsman and artist, and a paradise for children. T 01326 252200. Open daily, all year from 10.
www.trebahgarden.co.uk

Tregrehan Gardens. Woodland garden created in the C19 by Carlyon family. Nursery. Camellias. Holiday cottages. T 01726 814389.

Open mid-Mar to end May, W-F, Su & BHMs 10.30-5, then W mid-June to end Aug, 1-4.30.
www.tregrehan.org

Tremenheere Sculpture Gardens, Nr Gulval. This is a relatively new venture that opened in 2012, and all is set in a sheltered valley with stupendous views across the Bay. Within the woods, streams and sub-tropical plantings are sculptures. The Lime Tree café (tapas and bar) provides the food, and is, in themselves a worthy destination,. T 01736 448089 Open East M to early Sept M-Sa 10-5, Su 10-4.
www.tremenheere.co.uk

Trevarno Estate Gardens & National Museum of Gardening. An unforgettable experience, combining beautiful Victorian and Georgian gardens, with splendid Fountain Garden Conservatory, unique range of craft workshops, and Museum. T 01326 574274. Open daily, all year 10.30-5.
www.trevarno.co.uk

Trewidden Garden. Originally planted by T B Bolitho in the late C19, these 15-acres provide a profusion of colour, especially in Spring; bluebells, camellias, magnolias. T 01736 363021 Open late Feb to late Sept W-Su 10.30-5.30.
www.trewiddengarden.co.uk

Trewithen Gardens. 30-acre garden renowned for its magnificent collection of camellias, rhododendrons, magnolias and many rare trees and shrubs, surrounded by traditional parkland landscaped in the C18. New sculpture fountain. T 01726 883647. Gardens open Mar-Sept M-Sa 10-4.30. Su Mar-May only. House open M & Tu Apr-July, & Aug BH M 2-4.
www.trewithengardens.co.uk

Trebah Gardens in Spring ss

Roskilly's, St Keverne

Camel Valley Vineyards. Award-winning wines from 8,000 vines grow on a south-facing valley. Tastings, shop (10-5) and pre-booked tours at 2.30 and 5pm W; T 01208 77959. Open East-Oct M-F 2-5, some W/Es. Holiday cottages.
www.camelvalley.com

Callestock Cider Farm. 40 varieties of fruit products, from scrumpies to chutneys. Farm animals and tractor rides. Guided tour of museum, distillery and underground cellars. Restaurant. T 01872 573356. Open all year M-F 9-5.
www.thecornishcyderfarm.co.uk

Cornish Orchards, Westnorth Manor Farm. Hand-crafted apple juices and ciders from over 1,000 of the Old Cornish variety of apple tree. Open all year, M-F 10-5, Sa 9.30-12.30. T 01503 269007.
www.cornishorchards.co.uk

Curgurrell Farm, Portscatho. The farmer, Simon Taffinder, is Portscatho's Harbour Master who owns a bevy of lobster and crab pots. He can also provide fresh fish caught on the line; mackerel, bass, plaice, scallops, all caught within 6 miles of the farm. Open Apr-Oct M-Sa 10-12, 5-7 and daily in Dec 10-5. 01872 580243
www.curgurrellfarmshop.co.uk

Dairyland Farmworld. All-weather farm park with milking parlour, heritage centre, playground, nature trail and cream teas. Open daily late Mar to Oct 10-5 & School hols. T 01872 510246
www.dairylandfarmworld.com

Gear Farm Shop, St Martin's. The vegetables grown here are 90% organic. Bakery and Cafe. Roly's Fish sales outlet. Camping. T 01326 221150.

Old MacDonalds Farm, Porthcothan Bay. Designed for younger children where they can feed the pets, and enjoy pony rides, train rides, birds of prey, picnics, crazy golf, indoor play area and cafe. Camping. T 01841 540829. Open daily Apr-Oct 10-6.
www.oldmacdonalds.co.uk

Porteath Bee Centre, Nr Polzeath. Living honey bee exhibition behind glass. Honey products available on sale and cream teas. Pooh Corner for kids. Shop open daily all year 10.30-4.30. Exhibition East-Oct M-Sa. T 01208 863718.
www.poteathbeecentre.co.uk

Roskilly's. Working farm selling their farm produce; ice cream, fudge, clotted cream, preserves etc. Restaurant and tearoom. Furniture and glass gallery. Open daily 10-dusk (W/Es in winter). Footpaths through woods, meadows and ponds. Holiday cottages. T 01326 280479.
www.roskillys.co.uk

Shire Horse Farm & Carriage Museum. A visit will take you back in time to a working farm with 15 shire horses and a display of horse-drawn vehicles. Wheelright and Blacksmith's shop. Free wagon rides, Cream teas. T 01209 713606 Open East to Sept 30, Su-F 10-6.

Trevathan Farm PYO. Strawberry farm with shop, restaurant and tearoom. Fruit in season. Pets corner. Fishing. Holiday cottages. Open daily from 9.30. T 01208 880164.
www.trevathanfarm.com

Tamar Valley Donkey Park. Cornwall's only donkey sanctuary with rides, indoor play area, pets and cafe. Open daily Apr-Sept 10-5.30, Oct Th-Su & W/Es Nov-Mar, except Jan. T 01822 834072.
www.donkeypark.com

Lobster, Curgurrel Farm

BIRDS & WILDLIFE

Cornish Birds of Prey Centre, Winnards Perch. Over 50 birds ranging from falcons, hawks and owls. Waterfowl Lake plus coarse fishing. Flights twice daily at 12 & 2.30. T 01637 880544. Open daily Apr-Oct 10-5.
www.cornishbirdsofprey.co.uk

Monkey Sanctuary, Looe. The first protected breeding colony of Amazon Woolly Monkeys in the world. Four species of Monkeys cared for. Bat Cave & Wildlife Room. Tree Top Cafe for refreshments. Open Apr-Sept Su-Th 11-4.30. T 01503 262532.
www.monkeysanctuary.org

National Seal Sanctuary, Gweek. The Sanctuary is a permanent home for seals and sealions unable to return to the wild. It also rescues, rehabilitates and releases seal pups from around our coasts back into the wild. There are Feeding Talks throughout the day, Nature Trail Walk, Seal Hospital, Nursery, Convalescent and Resident Pools. Open daily from 10.
www.sealsanctuary.co.uk

Blue Reef Aquarium, Newquay's Towan Beach. This overlooks one of England's most popular surf beaches and houses the creatures which live beneath those crashing and tickling, waves! Journey through a wonderland of underwater worlds, from the Cornish coastline, to the undersea gardens of the Mediterranean. Cafe/gift shop. Open daily from 10. T 01637 878134.
www.bluereefaquarium.co.uk/newquay

Newquay Zoo, Trenance Gardens. 10 acres of exotic gardens; Tropical House, Village Farm, Hedgehog Hospital, Dragon maze, children's play area. Many endangered species. Picnics. Cafe. Open daily Apr-Oct 9.30-6, Nov-Mar 10-5. T 01637 873342. (G7)
www.newquayzoo.org.uk

National Lobster Hatchery, Padstow. A Visitor Centre and research their laboratories promote the conservation and management of coastal marine resources. Open daily, all year from 10. T 01841 533877.
www.nationallobsterhatchery.co.uk

Monkey Sanctuary Trust, Looe ss

Paradise Park. A well-establshed wildlife conservation sanctuary, with 400 birds and animals, in 100 aviaries in a 7-acre garden. Indoor play area. "Eagles of Paradise" flying displays. World Parrot Trust. Cornish Otter Sanctuary. Open daily summer 10-5, winter 10-4. T 01736 753365.
www.paradisepark.org.uk

Porfell Wildlife Park & Sanctuary. Designed for all ages to enjoy domestic and exotic wild animals; ocelots, wallabies, meerkats, lemurs, iguanas with play area and walks in fine countryside. Open daily Apr-Oct 10-6. T 01503 220211.
www.porfellanimalland.co.uk

Screech Owl Sanctuary. Rescue and rehabilitation centre for sick and injured owls. Guided tours. Tearoom. Open daily Apr-Oct 10-6, winter 10-4. T 01726 860182.
www.screechowlsanctuary.co.uk

Tamar Ottter Sanctuary. The World's leading Otter conservation organisation that breeds and regularly introduces young otters into the wild. Set in 20 acres of mature woodland where three species of deer roam free, and where British and Asian Otters live in large semi-natural enclosures. Waterfowl lakes, nature trail and picnic area. Teas/gifts. T 01566 785646. Open daily, Apr-Oct, 10.30-6.

You May Also Like to Consider:-

Fowey Aquarium, Town Quay. Wide collection of marine life set beneath the Town Hall which dates back to 1793. Open daily May-Dec 10-5.

Grey Seal, St Ives Harbour

COUNTRY RESERVES & PLACES OF NATURAL INTEREST

Bodmin Moor. A wild and remote landscape, of sudden mists and mysterious legend. A vegetation of boggy moorland, open heathland, granite tors and hidden valleys. The highest point is Brown Willy (1,377ft). This remote wilderness, far from the dangerous beasts of the forest and plains, attracted prehistoric man. Hut circles, burial grounds and stone circles litter the landscape. An exhilarating place for pony trekking and walking, but beware of sudden mists!

Carrick Roads. 4-mile long drowned valley, fed by 5 tributaries. Boat trips from Falmouth to Truro and St Mawes from Prince of Wales, Pier. At Custom House Quay, trips to Helford Passage and Roseland in summer season. Popular with Yachtsmen.

Combe Valley Nature Trail. This trail starts at Combe Cottages, to follow a green and peaceful wooded valley, rich in oakwoods, honeysuckle and birdlife - buzzards, woodpeckers, dippers. Nearby, Stowe Barton, home of Sir Richard Grenville, County Sheriff of Cornwall in 1577 who was immortalised in Tennyson's poem The Revenge.

Floe Creek. Haven for wildfowl and herons. Start of 6 1/2 mile walk around peninsula, to Towan Beach, coast path to Zone Point, Carricknath Point, St Anthony and back. Shorter 3 1/2 mile walk, Westwards direct to Porthmellin Head and St Anthony.

Fowey River. Rises on Bodmin Moor, and is especially beautiful between Lostwithiel and Doublebois where it runs beside richly wooded riverbanks. Fly Fishing for brown trout and sea trout is possible. A fine spot to explore is from the Golitha Falls where a trail starts at Redgate Bridge. Follow the riverbank, and wonder at the profusion of wild flowers, to a tranquil resting place.

Tamar Otter Sanctuary ss

Goonhilly Downs. The high central plateau of the Lizard Peninsula, and of great interest to botanists, geologists and archaeologists. It has a profusion of wild flowers where the summer air is acute with scent. Buzzards soar up high. Green serpentine rock forms. Croft Pascoe Nature Reserve.

Helford River. Beautiful tree-lined tidal river with romantic creeks (Frenchman's Creek), and picturesque villages of Durgan and Helford. Popular with 'muck abouters' in boats. Oyster farm at Porth Navas.

Loe Pool. The largest natural lake in the West Country inhabited by wildfowl, and surrounded by rhododendrons and wild flowers. In evidence since the C14, the River Cober was blocked by silt and the Loe Bar developed to form a bank of flint shingle.

Luxulyan Valley. Wooded ravine overgrown with flowers and fauna. Watered by nearby clay pit.

St Nectan's Glen, Nr Tintagel. The C5 hermitage of St Nectan. This is considered one of Cornwall's most sacred sites, and a place of beauty and tranquillity. You may visit St Nectan's Kieve, a 60ft waterfall, and the Hermitage Tea Gardens. Open daily East-Oct 10.30-6.30. www.stnectan.currantbun.com

You May Also Like to Consider:

Tamar Lakes Wildlife Refuge, Nr Kilkhampton. Two large lakes where you may fish for rainbow trout, and coarse fish, and hire rowing boats.

Valency Valley, Nr Boscastle. Two-hour walk up dreamlike valley through woodland to St Juliot's Church where Thomas Hardy met his first wife Emma Gifford, the vicar's sister.

Newquay Zoo ss

Botallack Engine House

The Cornish landscape is haunted by silhouettes of chimneys and engine houses on the skyline, and by ramshackle desolate buildings beside the road. The remains of a once prosperous tin and copper mining industry. Most examples to be found in the Camborne to Redruth area, and on the Penwith Peninsula. Restored by the National Trust and other bodies. They stand in spectacular positions, and are worthy of a visit. The better known are: Wheal Coates, Engine House, Nr St Agnes and, Wheal Prosper Copper Mine, Nr Porthleven. Please Note: In areas of former mining activity, it is imperative that one keeps to the evident pathways. Walkers and their dogs have been known to disappear down hidden shafts.

Blue Hills Tin Streams. Generations of miners have applied their trade here, from mining the valley floor, to tunnelling into the hillside. Guided tours of the skills of the ancient tinner; from rock to metal. Giftware. Open Apr-Oct M-Sa 10-2. T 01872 553341. www.bluehillstin.com

Botallack Engine Houses. The haunting and terrifying remains of the famous tin mine, operational from 1720-1914, which employed 500 people. Tunnels and galleries were projected beneath the sea. The roaring Atlantic clearly audible above the miners' heads. In 1893 the roof collapsed drowning 29 men, 500 feet down, never to be recovered. NB Please keep to paths. www.trevithick-society.org.uk

Camborne School of Mines Geological Museum, Pool. World-wide collection of minerals in school founded in 1888. Exhibition by local artists. Open M-F 10-4. www.uec.ac.uk/csm

Delabole Slate Quarry. This is some quarry, with a 1 1/2 mile circumference at a depth of 500ft, and 375 million years of geological history. It is impressive and has been worked continuously since the C16, possibly by the Romans. Tours of Quarry from May-Aug, M-F from 2pm. T 01840 212242. www.delaboleslate.co.uk

Dolcoath Mine. At 3,500 ft below the surface, Cornwall's deepest mine. Shut down in 1921 following the tin slump after WW1.

Geevor Tin Mining Heritage Centre. Set within the largest preserved mining site in the UK. A working mine until 1990, now a museum with tours of the surface plant and underground (12 & 2pm). Museum, film show, cafe and shop. Open Su-F from 9, underground tours from 10, last admission in summer 4, in winter 3. T 01736 788662. www.geevor.com

Gwennap Pit, Near St Day. This amphitheatre was created by mining subsidence, or divine intervention (depending on your point of view). It was landscaped in 1803 to fine tune excellent acoustics, and is known as the Methodist 'Cathedral'. John Wesley first preached here in 1762, and in 1773, to a congregation of 32,000! Annual Methodist Meeting - spring BHM. Visitor Centre open Spring BH M to 30 Sept M-F 10-4.30, Sa 10-1.

Huel Vor. Cornish for 'Great Work'. A disused mine with 30 foot wide seams worked at depths of 2,500 ft.

Mineral Tramways Discovery Centre, King Edward Mine, Troon. Cornwall's industrial past is revealed on two-wheels along the Portreath Tramroad of 11km and the Great Flat Lode trails of10km. Both great bike routes. Interpretation Centre. T 01209 614681. Open all year Tu-Su 10-4, Sa 1-4 .

Poldark Mine. A World Heritage Site where you can follow in the footsteps of C18 tin miners along underground passages with easy, and difficult, routes. Suitable for the elderly, the fit and fearless. Poldark Museum and film. Surface fun for the family. T 01326 573173. Open East-Oct Su-F 10-5.30, & Sa in summer hols. www.poldark-mine.co.uk

Gwennap Pit

Engine House, Troon

Royal Albert Bridge, Saltash

INDUSTRIAL INTEREST

Calstock Viaduct. 12 arch viaduct built to carry railway wagons from local mines to Calstock Quay. Whereby, the wagons were raised, and lowered, in a lift.

Carnglaze Slate Caverns & The Rum Store. Famous subterranean lake with crystal clear blue-green water in three huge underground chambers of cathedral-like proportions. Guided tours. Rock and classical music concerts. T 01209 714866. Open all year M-Sa 10-5. www.carnglaze.bt.com

Goonhilly Earth Station. International communication centre dealing with satellite and undersea cable links, to and from, around the globe. Transmitting and receiving millions of phone calls, TV pictures, news stories, fax and computer data. The Visitor Centre remains closed. wwwgoonhily.bt.com

Land's End Aerodrome, St Just. Pleasure flights over Land's End. Flying school. Schedule services to Scilly Isles. T 01736 788771. Open daily 9-6. www.landsendairport.co.uk

Marconi Monument. The first transatlantic Morse Code messages were transmitted from this spot on 12 December 1901, and picked up by Gugliemo Marconi in St Johns, Newfoundland.

Porthcurno Telegraph Museum. Secret wartime communication centre built in tunnels. Cable ships and cable-laying. T 01736 810966. Open daily Apr to early Nov, & winter Su & M, 10-5. www.porthcurno.org.uk

Goonhilly Earth Station ss

Royal Albert Bridge, Saltash. This beautiful, "Bowstring Suspension Bridge" is an iron single-track railway bridge built by I K Brunel in 1859. His last great feat of engineering. The design comprises of a wrought iron tubular arch or bow, in the form of a parabola, in a combination with sets of suspension chains hanging on each side of the tube in a catenary curve. www.royalalbertbridge.co.uk

St Austell Brewery. Traditional brewers since 1869. Guided tours, and beer sampling, at 11am and 2.30pm. Licensed shop. Open M-F 9.30-4.30. T 01726 66022 www.staustellbrewery.co.uk

Bodmin & Wenford Railway ss

Tregonning Hill. William Cookworthy, a Plymouth chemist discovered Kaolin here in 1768, a substance which is the basis of England's porcelain industry. Later, extensive finds were discovered around Hensbarrow Downs. St Austell grew to become the centre of the industry. Kaolin is a product of changed granite; the rock is extracted from enormous pits, 300ft deep and 1/2 mile across. Only a portion is utilised, the remainder is piled in great white heaps, hundreds of feet high, like towering snow mountains, the 'Cornish Alps' on which vegetation scarcely grows (unless the Alp is part of the Eden Project).

Wheal Martyn China Clay Country Park, Nr St Austell. Set in 26 acres of woodland on the outskirts of St Austell. Both the historic and the nature trails provides an insight into the development of this important Cornish Industry. Picnic and children's play area. Coffee shop. Open daily, all year from 10 (closed M in winter). www.wheal-martyn.com

RAILWAYS & CANALS

Bodmin & Wenford Railway, Bodmin General Station. Step back into the nostalgic 1940s with a 13-mile round trip on a standard gauge steam railway through the beautiful Cornish countryside. Trains run from 10.30 on selected dates (daily late May to early Oct). T 01208 73666 for details. www.bodminandwenfordrailway.co.uk

Bude's Old Canal. Built in 1819-26 at a length of 43 miles (61km). For 60 years used to transport coal and lime inland, and to export grain and slate. Killed off by other railways. Best sections are at Marhamchurch, Hobbacott Down and Werrington. www.bude-canal.co.uk

Cotehele Quay (NT). Picturesque C18 and C19 buildings beside the River Tamar. A small out-station of the National Maritime Museum, and berth for the restored Tamar sailing barge, 'Shamrock', a 57 foot ketch-rigged vessel that plied its trade hereabouts, in times gone by, and you can board it on Sundays. Museum, Art and craft gallery and tearoom. Open daily Apr-Oct. www.nationaltrust.org.uk

Lappa Valley Railway & Leisure Park. Steam railway giving a two mile return trip along a 15' gauge line to a pleasure area with boating lakes, crazy golf, maze, children's railway, walks and film show. Cafe and gift shop. T 01872 510317. Open daily East-Oct & 1/2 term 10.30-5.30. Santa Specials in Dec. www.lappavalley.co.uk

Launceston Steam Railway. Two-foot gauge steam railway using Victorian locomotives along a beautiful country line. After 2 1/2 miles, Newmills Station, access to farm park. Transport and Industrial Museum with working exhibits. Cafe, shop and bookshop. T 01566 775665. Open East week, Spring BH & Oct 1/2 term, June Su M & Tu, July-Sept Su-F, 10.30-4.30. www.launcestonsr.co.uk

World of Model Railways, Mevagissey. Over 2,000 models, 30 trains controlled in sequence. Model shop. T 01726 842457. Open daily late Mar to Oct & winter W/Es, from 10. www.model-railway.co.uk

Lappa Valley Railway ss >

Barbara Hepworth Museum & Sculpture Garden

MUSEUMS

Barbara Hepworth Museum & Sculpture Garden, Barnoon Hill, St Ives. The house, studio, sculpture garden and workshop of the late Sculptress. 40 sculptures, paintings and photographs. T 01736 796226. Open all year Tu-Su 10-4.20 and daily Mar-Oct 10-5.20.
www.tate.org.uk/stives/hepworth

Bodmin Museum, Mount Folly. Exhibits of local history, Victorian Kitchen. 'Echoes of Bodmin Moor!'. T 01208 77067. Open East-Sept M-F 10.30-4.30 (Sa 2.30), Oct 10.30-2.30.

Mevagissey Folk Museum, East Quay. Exhibits of local origin; fishing, agriculture and domestic life in an old 1745 building where Luggers (fishing boats) were built. T 01726 843568. Open daily East-Oct 11-4 (-5 July/Aug).
www.mevagisseymuseum.co.uk

Mlitary Museum, The Keep, Bodmin. Weapons, medals, uniforms, badges and military history based on the Duke of Cornwall's Light Infantry. Open M-F 10-5, Su in July/Aug 10-4.
www.lightinfantry.org.uk/regiments/dcli/duke_museum

National Maritime Museum, Discovery Quay, Falmouth. Historic collection of British and international boats. Designed "To promote an understanding of boats and their place in people's lives, to inspire new boat design and to promote an understanding of the maritime heritage of Cornwall." T 01326 313388. Open daily 10-5.
www.nmmc.co.uk

Padstow Museum, Market Place. Maritime and local interest; 'Obby' oss, lifeboat, fishing, old Music Rolls and more. T 01841 532752. Open East to Oct M-F 10.30-4.30, Sa 10.30-1.
www.padstowmuseum.co.uk

Paul Corin's Magnificent Music Machines. The Marquis of Campden's 1912 Aeolian Pipe Organ, orchestrions and the Mighty Wurlitzer Theatre Organ. T 01579 343108. Open daily Good F-Oct 10.30-5.
www.paulcorinmusic.co.uk

Royal Cornwall Museum, River Street, Truro. World-famous collection of minerals, archaeology, ceramics, paintings and Old Master drawings. Archives and ephemera relating to Cornwall and the South West with extensive collection of photographs from 1845. T 01872 272205. Open Tu-Sa 10-4.45. (G9)
www.royalcornwallmuseum.org.uk

Shipwreck and Heritage Centre, Charlestown. The largest shipwreck artefact collection in the UK. Titanic display. Hands-on rescue equipment and lots more. T 01726 69897. Open daily Mar-Oct 10-5.
www.shipwreckcharlestown.com

Wayside Folk Museum, Zennor. This, the oldest, privately owned museum in Cornwall, houses 12 themed areas, all set within a magical C16 Miller's cottage. There are over 5,000 artefacts to discover. Cornish crafts, bookshop and riverside tea garden. Open daily Apr-Oct 11-5 (May-Sept 10.30-5.30).
www.zennor.org/wayside_museum.html

National Maritime Museum, Falmouth ss

Neil Pinkett, Cornwall Contemporary ss

ART GALLERIES

Cornwall Contemporary, 1 Parade St., Penzance. A leading, independent gallery run by Sara Brittain who has had a long and happy association with West Country artists. Open M-Sa 10-5.
www.cornwallcontemporary.com

Falmouth Art Gallery, The Moor. Maritime pictures and quality temporary exhibitions. Works by Alfred Munnings, Frank Brangwyn, J W Waterhouse and Henry Scott Tuke. Open all year M-Sa 10-5.
www.falmouthartgallery.com

Glass House Gallery, 81-82 Market Jew Street, Penzance. A serious and attractive gallery exhibiting paintings, ceramics, sculpture and jewellery with regular changing shows. T 01736 367619
www.glasshousegallery.co.uk

Lemon Street Gallery, Truro. A gallery whose aim is to introduce the British Art Scene to Cornwall. Modern and Contemporary art, sculpture and ceramics. Open M-Sa 10.30-5.30.
www.lemonstreetgallery.co.uk

Market House Gallery, The Square, Marazion. This, the largest gallery in the village specialises in C20 Cornish artists and holds 6 exhibitions each year, of both one-person and group shows. Sculpture, glass and ceramics are also displayed. Open daily. T 01736 719019
www.markethousegallery.co.uk

Mid Cornwall Galleries, St Blazey Gate. Some of the finest of contemporary British Art and Crafts; paintings, ceramics, silks, glass, jewellery. Open Feb-Dec M-Sa 10-5, Jan 11-4.
www.midcornwallgalleries.co.uk

New Millennium Gallery, Street-an-Pol, St Ives. A leading gallery with contemporary paintings and ceramics at the leading edge, in a three-storey building. Open Mar-Oct M-Sa 10-5.
www.millenniumgallery.co.uk

Newlyn Art Gallery, New Road. An enterprising, and at times, shocking art venue with changing exhibitions of painting, sculpture, drawing and photography. Installation and esoteric space is a concept practiced with panache, and endearment. Gallery shop. Open daily M-Sa 10-5.
www.newlynartgallery.co.uk

Penlee House Gallery & Museum, Morrab Road, Penzance. Paintings by the Newlyn School of Artists, plus social history and archaeology. Open daily M-Sa 10.30-4.30 Oct-Apr, May-Sept M-Sa 10-5.
www.penleehouse.org.uk

Stoneman Gallery, 56 Chapel St., Penzance. Linda is the widow of the Master Printer, Hugh Stoneman who worked with Terry Frost and others. This newish gallery reflects a classic view of modern and contemporary art forms. Open M-Sa 10.30-5.
www.stonemanpublications.co.uk

You May Also Like To Consider:

Tate St Ives, Porthmeor Beach. This is the first port-of-call for thousands who visit St Ives. They wish to walk in the shadow of Art and all its finery and pretension. Here you will discover displays of contemporary work in all variety of media. There are some very fine sculptures by Hepworth and a comprehensive show of St Ives' famous son, Alfred Wallis, fisherman and scrap merchant who didn't paint until he was 70! Worth a journey just for the view from the coffee shop and a visit to the bookshop. T 01736 796226. Open daily Mar-Oct 10-5.20, Nov-Feb Tu-Su 10-4.20. www.tate.org.uk/stives

The Exchange, Princes St., Penzance. Developed in conjunction with the Newlyn Art Gallery, this gallery showcases international art forms (sic), and holds regular educational programmes. Coffee shop. Open M-Sa 10-5. www.newlynartgallery.co.uk

The Great Atlantic, 48 Arwenack St., Falmouth. Impressive gallery in stunning building shows large canvases. Seasonal exhibitions. T 01326 318452. www.greatatlantic.co.uk/falmouth

The Lander Gallery, Lemon Street Market, Truro. Spacious open gallery displays C19 and C20 Cornish Masters to contemporary fine art and crafts. Coffee shop. Open M-Sa 9-6. www.landergallery.co.uk

Yew Tree Gallery, Morvah. Worth the journey to visit these converted stables facing the Atlantic, that puts on exhibitions of Applied and Fine Art. Sculpture and organic gardens. Open Tu-Sa 10.30-5.30, Su 2-5. www.yewtreegallery.com

The Cornubian Arts and Science Trust, 3 Penrose St., Helston. Cornwall's latest edition to the World of Art where studio spaces are occupied by a diverse range of artists. Open, as advertised on the door.

Kestle Barton, Manaccan, Helston. This is a new, community-based, arts centre with ever-changing exhibitions; painting, sculpture, ceramics, and events, all set within an ancient Cornish farmstead. Open Late Mar to Early Nov Tu-Sa 10.30-5. T 01326 231811 www.kestlebarton.co.uk

CRAFTSMANSHIP

Adrian Brough Pottery, Fore St., Lelant. Beautifully decorated pots of marine life, using ceramic styles from Portugal and Korea. Open M-F 9-5, W/Es by appoint. B&B. 01736 755515
www.adrianbroughpottery.co.uk

Leach Pottery, Upper Stennack, St Ives. Founded by Bernard Leach (d.1979) and Shoji Hamada in 1920, and arguably the most influential studio pottery in the world. A living tribute to Bernard Leach and his legacy. Open daily, all year from 10, Su from 11.
www.leachpottery.com

Malcolm Sutcliffe Glass Gallery, 2 West St., Penryn. Blown studio glass made on the premises by Malcolm Sutcliffe, plus jewellery, paintings and cards. Open W-F 11-5, Sa 10-1. T 01326 377020.
www.malcolm-sutcliffe.co.uk

Malcolm Sutcliffe Gallery ss

New Craftsman, 24 Fore St., St Ives. British Crafts Council Awards gallery celebrating 50+ years in business features ceramics, jewellery, glass, metalwork, and more. Open M-Sa 10-5.
www.newcraftsmanstives.com

Prindl Pottery, Nr Lanhydrock. Japanese inspired pots; some are of enormous size, and originality. Others, are simply shaped, in stoneware, or porcelain. Open M-F 10-5, W/Es by appoint.
www.prindlpottery.co.uk

St Ives Ceramics, Lower Fish St. Collections of high quality ceramics. Work by John Bedding, Clive Bowen, Bernard Leach and Japanese artists from Mashiko. Open daily 10-5.
www.st-ives-ceramics.co.uk

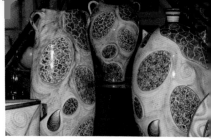

Adrian Brough, Round House Gallery, Sennen Cove

The Guild Of Ten, 19 Old Bridge St., Truro. Co-operative of craftsmen and women living in Cornwall. They seek to produce workmanship of the highest quality; knitwear, designer clothing, glass blowing, ceramics etc. Open M-Sa 9.30-5.30.
www.guildof10.co.uk

The Tyler Gallery, 12 Brook St., Mousehole. Established by Newlyn born potter Essex Tyler who specialises in ornamental raku pottery. The gallery also displays an impressive collection of Cornish paintings and jewellery. Open daily Mar-Dec 10-6. 01736 731109
www.tylergallery.co.uk

Trelissick Gallery. This is set within the National Trust's garden, and is run in partnership with the Cornwall Crafts Association to show off the best of Cornwall's arts and crafts. Open Feb-Dec M-Sa 10.30-5.30.
www.trelissickgallery.co.uk

Trelowarren Gallery. Original home of the Cornwall Crafts Association, now regularly holds members and touring exhibitions. Open Mar-Nov.
wwwcornwallcrafts.co.uk

Paul Jackson, The Guild of Ten ss

Flambards Experience ss

FAMILY FUN & ADVENTURE (FOR RAINY DAYS)

Arthurian Centre, Nr Camelford. Site of Arthurian legend and folk lore. Exhibition centre, woodland and river walks, tearoom and gift/bookshop. Play area. T 01840 213947. Open daily.
www.arthur-online.co.uk

Buccaneer Bay, Newquay. Life-size figures and scenes capture Cornwall's exciting and swashbuckling past: smugglers, giants, sea creatures, highwaymen, mermaids. T 01637 873379. Open East-Oct Su-F & BHs 10-dusk.
www.buccaneerbay.co.uk

Crealy Adventure Park, Nr Wadebidge. Mega-slides, twisters, water slides. Shire horses, farm museum with 120 acres to roam. Restaurant. T 01841 540276. Open Spring W/Es, then daily Apr to early Nov 10-5.
www.crealy.co.uk/cornwall

Flambards Experience, Helston. All-weather activities and attraction; Victorian Village and "Britain in the Blitz" experiences, Space Quest, live entertainment, Hands-On Science, Operation Sealion, and much more. Open most days Early Apr to end Oct 10.30-5.
www.flambards.co.uk

Hidden Valley Discovery Park, Nr Launceston. Adventure park and garden railway centre. Treasure hunts based around a shipwreck. Play area. Farm animals. Cafe. Two coarse fishing lakes. Open Apr-Sept Su-F & Aug Sa, 10.30-5.30.
www.hiddenvalleydiscoverypark.co.uk

Holywell Bay Fun Park, Nr Newquay. All action outdoor fun park; karts, battle and bumper boats, laser day pigeon shooting, cafe. T 01637 830095. Open daily East-Sept & Oct W/Es 10.30-5.
www.holywellbay.co.uk/funpark

Land's End. The Natural Landscape, plus 5 exhibitions including Arthur's Quest, Air Sea Rescue and End to End Story. Various craft workshops. Bar/Hotel. T 0870 4580044. Open all year 10-dusk.
www.landsend-landmark.co.uk

Springfields Fun Park & Pony Centre, Nr St Columb. Pets corner, bottle feeding, tractor rides and play areas. Indoor play barn. Cafe. Open daily Apr to Sept 10-6, Oct W/Es & 1/2 term 10-4.
www.springfieldsponycentre.co.uk

Trethorne Leisure Farm, Nr Launceston. Undercover family entertainment; milk a cow, bottle feed lambs, see chicks hatch. Ten pin bowling (open daily 10am-11pm), gladiator duels, drop-slide, astra-slide, restaurant, bar and shop. Farmhouse accommodation. T 01566 86324. Open daily 10-6.
www.trethorneleisure.com

Waterworld, Newquay. Fun pool, gym, dance and aerobic studio, sauna, solarium. skate park. T 01637 853828. Open daily.
www.newquaywaterworld.co.uk

Land's End

THEATRE

Halzephron Amphitheatre, Hazephron House, Gunwalloe. A varied mix of musical events have taken place, and are planned for, in the future. The situation is quite stunning as the backdrop is Mount's Bay, where the sun is forever setting. www.halzephronhouse.co.uk

Kneehigh Theatre Group, Walsingham Place, Truro. Through the conduit of The Asylum (a beautiful and nomadic structure), this group of players produce creative, thought-provoking, challenging and joyful productions to tease and entertain their audience. T 01872 267910 www.kneehigh.co.uk

Minack Open Air Theatre, Porthcurno. Open Air Theatre cut out of cliff side with season of plays, musicals and operas in a unique 750-seat theatre. Summer Season: May to mid-Sept. Exhibition Centre tells the story of Rowena Cade who built the theatre, open daily Apr to mid-Sept 9.30-5.30, winter from 10-dusk (closed 24/25 Dec). T 01736 810694. www.minack.com

St Piran's Round, Perranporth. An ancient amphitheatre where plays were performed in the C17.

Sterts Arts & Environment Centre. Lively programme of dance, music and theatre. Family picnics are ideal before each performance. Gallery and Workshops. Bistro and Bar. T 01579 362382. Open daily (theatre June-Sept) except Su. www.sterts.co.uk

The Poly, Falmouth. 24 Church St. 200 seat theatre (cinema) holds music, theatre and dance. Four galleries put on changing exhibitions. Cafe/bar. T 01326 319461. Open M-Sa 10-5. www.thepoly.org

The Rum Store, St Neot. Classical and pop concerts put on in the underground 400-seat auditorium at Carnglaze Caverns. The acoustics are considered to be top class. T 01579 320251. www.carnglaze.com

The Tolmen Centre, Constantine. A varied arts programme is organically created out of this little build; from movie-making, to plays, to choir-making. There are also vibrant courses of yoga, Pilates and Todlins. T 01326 341353

The Three Musketeers, Minack Theatre ss

Abbey Hotel ss

Abbey Hotel, Penzance. This sweet gem dating from the C17 stands hidden behind a walled garden, and courtyard. It has been lovingly decorated with an array of fabrics awash with colour. You may call it shabby chic, or an antique emporium. The owner is the former fashion icon, Miss Jean Shrimpton, rarely here, usually at home in Windsor. This little hotel will leave you with fond memories. It is different. T 01736 366906 www.theabbeyonline.co.uk

Bedruthan Steps Hotel. One of Cornwall's great family hotels set high on the cliff's edge overlooking Mawgan Porth beach. Awarded a Green Tourism Gold Award. It uses solar panels and light sensors, helps clean the local beach and uses local suppliers. T 01637 860555 www.bedruthan.com

Driftwood Hotel, Portscatho. If you find yourself, by chance, washed up here on the shore then you are in luck. It is, as described, decorated in pieces of driftwood. This washes over you to create a laidback ambience where you can look out over the sea, enjoy the garden and hospitality. Perhaps, find the path to the private beach. Food is accomplished. Bedrooms contemporarily funished and light. No dogs. T 01872 580644 www.driftwoodhotel.co.uk

Fowey Hall Hotel, Fowey. This is what has been described as a luxurious family hotel. You will see lots of children making lots of noise, but rarely with their parents, because the nannies are in tow. The Father's are hidden in corners stuck to their mobile 'phones. This is an expensive nursery. Kids paintings adorn the walls. Dogs and Grandmothers are allowed to venture here, too. It is exclusive, and is not cheap. You may ask; Are the parents allowed to dine alone? T 01726 833866 www.foweyhallhotel.co.uk

Stein's Seafood Restaurant ss

The Scarlet ss

Greenbank Hotel, Falmouth. This is the town's oldest and most respected hotel that has undergone a massive refurbishment. It caters for all manner of life; romantic breaks, weddings, corporate. It is in the business of hospitality. It also has some sweeping views over the harbour. T 01326 312440
www.greenbank-hotel.co.uk

Hotel Tresanton, St Mawes. This is a chic, family-friendly hotel that has raised the bar by which all are judged in Cornwall, and elsewhere. It is owned by the interior designer, Olga Polizzi (Forte) and her husband, the political commentator, William Shawcross. Ms Polizzi has understated good taste in bucketfuls. She manages to marry comfort with contemporary art, and antiques. She pulls it off, spectacularly. Nothing is too cluttered, and you know that the objects: sculptures, artworks, furniture, have been sort for, visualised, and positioned in situ, well in advance of your visit. Seafood is a speciality, surprise, surprise. T 01326 270055
www.tresanton.com

Lugger Hotel, Portloe. This was formerly a C17 smugglers inn. Well disposed to catch fresh fish and lobster directly off the local boats. It has been transformed into a chic, comfortable hotel, noted for its fine dining and romantic al fresco moments. T 01872 501322
www.luggerhotel.com

Rick Stein's, Padstow. If you wish to guarantee a table at Mr Stein's formidable hostelry then try one of these. They have 40 plush bedrooms scattered around Padstow; in the Seafood Restaurant, St Petroc's Hotel, St Edmunds House, Rick Stein's Café, Bryn Cottage and Prospect House. All have crisp linen, superb bathrooms and indulgent beds. The ultimate Restaurant With Rooms experience. T 01841 532700
www.rickstein.com

St Enodoc Hotel, Rock. This is a family-friendly hotel, noted for its great location, cuisine, gym and spa. It is especially devoted to families of all ages, and the new décor is bright, comfy, colourful, and very seasidie. Special Breaks. The restaurant is managed by the Trencherman, Nathan Outlaw, often described as one of Cornwall's finest culinary masters. T 01208 863394
www.enodoc-hotel.co.uk

St Moritz, Trebetherick. This is a quite recent development; hotel, apartments and a spa complex providing all manner of amenities that one (if you visit such places of hedonism) would expect from such a venture: gym, indoor pool, saunas etc., bar, games room and more. T 01208 862242
www.stmoritzhotel.co.uk

You May Also Like To Consider:

The Old Quay House Hotel, Fowey. If you, like me, consider estuaries to be chilled, calming; the ebb and flow of the tide, boats at anchor, whistling halyards, bliss... continual interest, and when the views are stunning, you have a match made in...? The rooms are bright and pleasing, and the al fresco dining is a delight. T 01726 833302
www.theoldquayhouse.com

The Scarlet, Mawgan Porth. Eco, green, sustainable living...pure hedonism. This is what separates this multi-million pound investment from its peers. Is there a paradox? It is an expensive place to play and relax....a pity that their example has yet translate into cheaper, more plentiful options. No children. T 01637 861800
www.scarlethotel.co.uk

BED & BREAKFAST

Buttervilla Farm, Polbathic. An eco-friendly, organic farm of 15 acres. The dècor is contemporary, and comfortable, the showers are solar heated. Dinner is by arrangement. Most vegetables are home grown. Wi-fi access. T 01503 230315
www.buttervilla.com

Ednovean Farm, Perranuthnoe. This is what the Pros call luxury B&B. Three gorgeous bedrooms decorated in designer fabrics with immaculate bathrooms. All surrounded by an exquisite Italian garden. Are you seduced? T 01736 711883
www.ednovean.co.uk

Ennys, St Hilary. This is a perfectly proportioned Cornish farmhouse just off the beaten track. All laid to flagstone floors, square rooms and high ceilings. The artworks and books reflect the multi-travels of your hostess. Self-catering cottages. T 01736 740262
www.ennys.co.uk

Gardens Cottage, Prideaux. Sometimes you come across a B&B that feels just right, and you don't want to leave. Hidden away in the Luxulyan Valley is Kath and Ivan Walker's exceptional and charming cottage with all the creature comforts you will ever need, and much more. T 01726 817195
www.gardenscottage.co.uk

Ednovean Farm ss

Halzephron House

Halzephron House, Gunwalloe. "The Views Are To Live And Die For." This was quite a statement by a literary visitor, and his friends (AA Milne, JM Barrie, et al). Few would argue with them. Halzephron looks over Mount's Bay, and is crossed by the coastal footpath. The rooms are described as contemporary, quirky, arty, the breakfasts are foodie-specials. A pub is within walking distance. There is also the Cabin, for two romantics. It is a place where dreams are made. T 07899 925816
www.halzephronhouse.co.uk

Hen House, Tregarne. If you seek solitude and meadows of wild flowers and wish to escape from this mad world, the Hen House maybe just the place for you. Self-catering barn. No children U-12. T 01326 280236
www.thehenhouse-cornwall.co.uk

Lantallack Farm, Landrake. Grade II Georgian farmhouse provides large, comfy bedrooms and organic breakfasts. Your hostess, Nicky, is an artist, and will teach you printmaking, painting and sculpture. T 01752 851281
www.lantallack.co.uk

Little Roseland B&B, Treworga. A delightful, C18 Cornish house, surrounded by an enchanting garden. Your hostess, Didi Vernon Miller has brought all her interior design skills to bear on the gorgeous bedrooms. T 01872 501243
www.littleroseland.co.uk

Reddivallen, Trevalga. Farmhouses don't come more solid than this one. It's straight out of Poldark! The Brewers breed fine Hereford cattle and produce organic beef on their 300-acre farm. The bedrooms are bright and comfortable enjoying splendid views. T 01840 250854
www.redboscastle.com

Shamrock Cabin, Whitsand Bay. Kick off your shoes and play at being shipwrecked in this perfectly formed log cabin atop the cliffs at Whitsand Bay. Nothing ahead of you, but an endless sea view. All you need in the cabin, and the Clifftop Café and View Restaurant, all within walking distance. Leave the car keys in the suitcase and let your cares drift away. Sleeps 2. www.shamrockcabin.co.uk

You May Also Like To Consider:

The House In the Sea, Newquay. If you fancied a romantic interlude on your own private island then this location with breath-taking views may be just for you. Luxuriously decorated, and surrounded by the sea at High Tide. Sleeps 2. Civilization is reached via a 70ft-high suspension bridge. T 01637 881942 www.houseinthesea.uniquehomestays.com

The Old Rectory, St Juliot. This is where Thomas Hardy (poet and novelist) met his beloved Emma Gifford who later became his wife, and where he returned on her death to write some of his greatest poetry. If you seek a luxurious B&B with Green credentials and literary connections, none better. T 01849 250225 www.stjuliot.com

The Old Vicarage, Morwenstow. To gauge the RS Hawker Experience you must stay here in his former home. Your hosts are a mine of information. Comfortable B&B with platefuls of home cooking. Carrow's Stable to let. T 01288 331369 www.rshawker.co.uk

BUDGET BEDS/CAMP SITES

Cornish Tippi Holidays, Tregeare. Something different. Hire a traditional North American tent amidst a haven of birdsong, wild flowers, buzzards and rabbits. Trout fishing. No cars on site. Warden on hand. T 01208 880781 www.cornishtipiholidays.co.uk

Goofys, 5 Headland Rd., Newquay. This is a boutique-surf hostel with some style within close proximity of Britain's finest surf beaches. Can accommodate 14 guests, in 6 rooms. T 01637 872684 www.goofys.co.uk

Henry's Campsite, The Lizard. If you wanted to introduce your kids (or your wife, for that matter) to camping, then start here. Close to the village and coastal path. The situ is rural, and the camping is your max 4-berth tent. Everything else is exotic; from the plants, to the Easter Island décor, to the poultry. T 01326 290596 www.henryscampsite.co.uk

Kelynack Caravan & Camping Park, St Just. A small, well-run and friendly site that also offers mobile homes and B&B. T 01736 787633 www.kelynackholidays.co.uk

Cornish Tippi Holidays ss

No 11 Fore Street, St Just. Cosy cottage B&B with 2 double-rooms. Perfect for hikers and surfers for they will forward baggage and provide pack lunches. T 01736 786767 www.11forestreet.co.uk

North Shore Bude, 57 Killerton Rd. A specialist surf hostel with 12 rooms to choose from; ideal for family parties, couples and groups on a budget. T 01288 354256 www.northshorebude.com

Ruthern Valley Holidays. Nestling in a wooded valley this site offers traditional facilities for tents and caravans but also log cabins, wigwams, camping huts and bungalows. www.ruthernvalley.com

Treen Farm, St Levan. This is first come, first served from 8.00 am. It is tranquil, and open to the full force of the elements. Great when the weather is calm. Ideal for climbers, walkers, naturists, and dog lovers. T 07598 469322 www.treenfarmcapmsite.co.uk

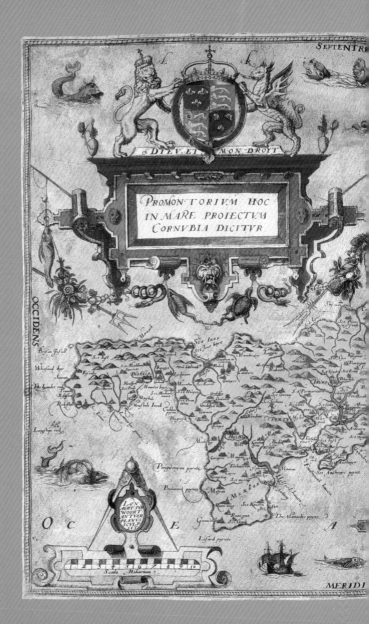

SEPTENTR

OCCIDENS

DIEV ET MON DROYT

PROMONTORIVM HOC
IN MARE PROIECTVM
CORNVBIA DICITVR

TREVS

PER

MERID

MERIDI

O c E A

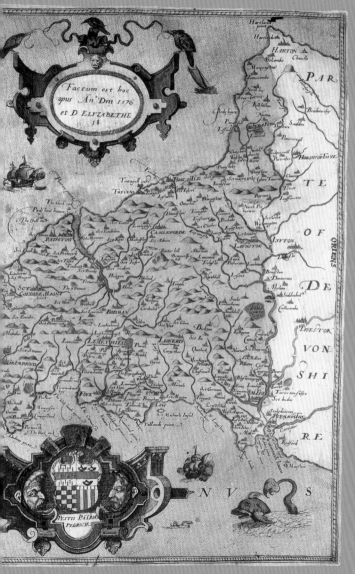

Factum est hoc
opus An° Dm 1576
et D. ELIZABETHE
18

PUBS SERVING FOOD

Cornish Arms, St Merryn. This pub is now part of the Rick Stein and St Austell Brewery empires. During the renovation of this old pub I couldn't help noticing the number, and enormous size, of the septic tanks being lowered into the ground. The owners planned for volume sales, and I believe, achieve it. The food offered is simple British pub menu; real beef burgers, mussels, chips and scampi in a basket. Beer garden. No reservations. Visit the Church, opposite.
www.rickstein.com/The-Cornish-Arms

Gurnard's Head Hotel, Treen. The owners describe it as a Dining Pub. It will be a most welcome refuge if you have been battling against a sou'westerly head wind on the coastal footpath. The décor is classy and arty, the ambience is laid-back and the food will appease a mighty appetite, and empty your wallet. The bedrooms have Vi-Spring beds and dogs are welcome in the bar. T 01736 796928
www.gurnardshead.co.uk

Halzephron Inn, Gunwalloe. Well placed for an energetic walk along the coastal footpath, and or, a stopover to fuel a mighty appetite. This 500-year old inn is steeped in history; smuggling, shipwrecks, piracy. It overlooks Mounts Bay where a friendly, Cornish welcome will greet you. Daily Specials. B&B. T 01326 240406.
www.halzephron-inn.co.uk

Rising Sun Inn, Altarnun. Andy Mason has cooked in Michelin Star restaurants and, all over the World, and brings his enthusiasm and professionalism to this popular C16 pub on the edge of Bodmin Moor. A full range of ales is on hand. The décor is minimalist with Delabole slate, flagstone floors. Camping for tents and caravans, and well suited for cyclists, horse riders and walkers. T 01566 86636
www.therisingsuninn.co.uk

Roseland Inn, Philleigh-In-Roseland. This is a friendly, and often, crowded pub with log fires and low ceilings. A meeting point for friends from Falmouth, Truro and St Austell, and for pre-Wedding nerve, drinks – the church is close by. Pretty garden. Daily specials. Booking advised. Dogs and children welcome. T 01872 580254.
www.roselandinn.co.uk

Springer Spaniel, Treburley. A pub with a focus on food, especially Game in season, backed up by the owners parallel business - a 100 hectare organic farm rearing grass-fed, slowly matured South Devon cattle and Lleyn sheep. An eclectic mix of interior designs with log fires, a light and welcoming dining room, as well as a sheltered garden. Dogs and children welcome. T 01579 370424.
www.thespringerspaniel.org.uk

St Kew Inn. A village must have two essentials; a beautiful, historic church, and a cosy, relaxed pub within spitting distance of the former. St Kew proudly boasts both. It lies hidden away down narrow lanes, far away from the hurly-burly of Rock, and the Camel Estuary. The large garden is a popular lunchtime haunt. Specials board. T 01208 841259
www.stkewinn.co.uk

Pandora Inn

Rod and Line, Tideford

The Pandora, Restronguet Hill, Mylor Bridge. The setting has been described as magical, and the thatch build, a delight. It has all the ingredients for a splendid repast, and a quiet drink, either overlooking the calming waters of Restronguet Creek, or inside on a settle beside a log fire. Life doesn't get much better than this. Opens at 10.30 am. T 01326 372678
www.pandorainn.com

The Rod and Line, Tideford. If you yearn for a small, traditional pub, untainted by contemporary trends, but with the ambience of times gone by, and wish to sup from local fayre; crab, king prawns and scallops, and listen to musicians as varied as the late John Martyn or Chris Jagger, none better. T 01752 851323

Tinner's Arms, Zennor. This ancient and friendly pub brews its own ale, Tinners Ales, and serves quality nosh. The simple décor of settles and benches, and bonhomie makes it a delight just to sit here and enjoy the scene. Dogs and children welcomed.
www.tinnersarms.com

The White House, a Grade II listed building offering quality B&B. Known as Bos Cres ("house in the middle") there are two double-rooms and two single-rooms. WIFI. Packed lunches and luggage forwarding available. Small charge for dogs. T 01736 796927

You May Also Like To Consider:

Tolcarne Inn, Newlyn. Ben Tunnicliffe has taken over this old fisherman's pub, and is slowly building a name for himself (again). Formerly of the Abbey Restaurant, and The Scarlet, Ben is a master chef, and is a true exponent of Cornwall's rich and varied produce; the fish comes delivered, in person, by a footman, from Newlyn's Market, a mere hundred yards distant, and the veg and meat, are all locally produced, too. Brunch and coffee are served, and the coastal footpath passes the front door. Dog friendly. Live Jazz on Sundays 1-3pm. T 01736 363074
www.tolcarneinn.co.uk

Trengilly Wartha Inn, Nancenoy, Constantine. This busy pub has won countless awards for the quality of their beer and food, and lies hidden in a valley close to the Helford River. It has a bar, bistro, function room, garden and bedrooms, and a plentiful range of malt whiskys. Dog and cricketer, friendly. T 01326 340332
www.trengilly.co.uk

More Inns to consider for a refreshing pint of ale: Books & Beer, Bell Court (Falmouth), Blisland Inn (Blisland), Blue Anchor (Helston), Blue Peter Inn, (Polperro), Bush Inn (Morwenstow), Cadgwith Cove Inn (Cadgwith), Navy Inn (Penzance), The Lugger (Fowey), The Lugger (Polruan), The Ship Inn (Porthleven).

Ben Tunnicliffe, Tolcarne Inn

The Beach Hut, Watergate Bay

SEAVIEW CAFÉS/DINERS

Beach Hut, Watergate Bay. This is a child/family friendly café that provides fresh, simply cooked food when you need it most. And, when the last thing you want to do is cook for the family after a day in the surf. Fish and burgers feature, strongly. Daily Specials. Open from 8.30 till late. T 01637 860877
www.watergatebay.co.uk

The Castle Restaurant, The Wharf, Bude. Kit Davis would describe his establishment as a chic-café restaurant serving local produce with some flare and enthusiasm. You can also enjoy a romantic cocktail, and sea views from their splendid location. Opens at 10 am for coffee, 12 am for lunch and 6 pm for dinner. T 01288 350543
www.thecastlerestaurantbude.co.uk

Fifteen Cornwall, Watergate Bay. Another succes story for Jamie Oliver who helped set up Foundation Cornwall (Charity for Disadvantaged Children). Breakfast (first come, first served), lunch and dinner (require booking) served 7 days a week. The views are stupendous. The food, as you'd expect, is high quality. T 01637 86100.
www.fifteencornwall.co.uk

Godrevy Beach Café, Godrevy Towans. Serves breakfast, lunch and dinner. Choose from organic cakes, take-aways and barbecues. Sunset views from the decking area. Open from 10, all week. Further down the beach is the Sandsifters Bar on Gwithian Beach, for Apres-surf fun, pizzas, tapas and live music. Its teamed up with the Gwithian Academy of Surfing. T 01736 758384.
www.sandsiftervenue.com

Porthminster Beach Cafe, St Ives

Kota Kai Cafe, Porthleven

Kota Kai, The Harbour, Porthleven. The stunning view across the harbour will add spice to the fab food on offer; pasta, Asian, fish, mini-kai (tapas)… Open all day, especially for lunch and dinner. Kids Room. Next door, the Kota Restaurant for that "Special Occasion" dinner. Accomodation. T 01326 574411
www.kotakai.co.uk

Life's A Beach, Summerleaze Beach, Bude. Bistro offers all types of food, from locally caught fish to burgers and pizzas. In a breathtaking position to capture the sunset at day's end. Open daily in season. T 01288 355222
www.lifesabeach.info

Porthminster Beach Café. This blend of café and serious restaurant overlooking magical white sands has struck a chord with many foodie aficionados who consider it their First Choice diner in the South West. Child friendly. Open all year from 10 for morning coffee, lunch and dinner. Barbecue Bar for burgers and snacks, next door. Also, runs a sister café overlooking Porthmeor Beach, in front of Tate St Ives. 01736 795353
www.porthminstercafe.co.uk

The Beach, Sennen Cove. A view to live (and die) for. Restaurant built of wood and glass with black slate floors. Freshly prepared local produce. Al Fresco BBQs. Breakfast (in High Season) until 11.30. Light lunches 12-4.30, (teas) and supper 7-10. T 01736 871191.
www.thebeachrestaurant.com

The Edge, New Rd., Port Isaac. Smart bar and restaurant overlooks the sea. Contemporary art covers the walls. Specializes in local fish and meat dishes. Lunches, cream teas and dinner. T 01208 880090
www.theedge-cornwall.co.uk

The Polpeor Beach Café, The Lizard. This is a great spot to enjoy coffee, doughnuts and their home-baked cakes, as well as the aerial displays of the rare choughs. It is also England's most southern point where the gnarled and eroded rock forms hide a tumultuous past.

You May Also Like to Consider:

The View Restaurant, Trenninow Cliff Road, Rame Peninsula. Your first stop, and no better introduction to Cornwall. Classic French food with English produce. Child and Veggie friendly. Open for lunch and dinner. T 01752 822345
www.theview-restaurant.co.uk

The Watering Hole, Perranporth. Actually situated on the sand, backed by dunes and fronted by the sea. A great view if you can see past the basting hoards on the beach on sunny days. Feels like a little slice of Oz. T 01872 572888
www.the-wateringhole.co.uk

Life's A Beach, Bude

Thomas Flamank and Michael an Gof (Michael Joseph). Co-Leaders of the Cornish Rebellion of 1497; a lawyer, and a village blacksmith. Henry VII was fighting a war against the Scots and required funds. He raised taxes and these two believed, along with 15,000 rebels, that Cornwall could ill afford such sufferage. At Blackheath Common, poorly armed with bows, arrow, scythes and pitchforks were no match for the King's mercenaries. These two were found guilty of High Treason. Their punishment to be hung, drawn and quartered, and their heads displayed on London Bridge. In 1997 a statue was unveiled in St Keverne to commemorate the 500th Anniversary of these fine Cornishmen: "a name perpetual, and a fame permanent and immortal".

Sir Bevil Grenville, 1596-1643. Civil War Commander, Landowner, MP, Royalist. Born near Withiel, educated at Exeter College, Oxford. Knighted in 1639 having served in the King's bodyguard. He raised an army in Cornwall to fight for the King. Won battles at Braddock Down, Stratton Hill (Bude) and Lansdown outside Bath where he was mortally wounded. Buried in Kilkhampton Church. Monument erected in a field above Bath to commemorate his heroism and those of his Cornish Pikemen.

Jonathan Trelawney, 1650-1721. Catholic Zealot, Royalist, Scholar. Born in Pelynt. Educated at Westminster and Christ Church, Oxford. Bishop of Bristol, Exeter and finally, Winchester. Famous as one of the seven bishops who took umbrage at James II for his "Declaration of Indulgence" in 1682 which declared religious freedom in England.

John Opie, FRA, 1770-1807. Portrait Painter. Born near St Agnes. Apprenticed as a carpenter then discovered by Dr John Walcot who recognised his enormous potential and so taught him mathematics and science. Opie's style was considered similar to Rembrandt's, and for twenty years he was London Society's most sort after portrait painter. He was appointed Professor of Painting at the Royal Academy. He died young and lies buried in St Paul's Cathedral.

Richard Trevithick, 1771-1833. Inventor, Mining Engineer. Born at Tregajorran near Camborne. He became one of the leading figures and a pioneer of the Industrial Revolution. His inventions included the High Pressure Steam Engine, Floating Docks, London Steam Carriage, Ship's Propeller, Iron Tanks, Water-Jet Propulsion, Thames Dredger, Portable Stoves, Threshing Machine and Railway Locomotives. He died of pneumonia in Dartford, in extreme poverty.

Henry Trengrouse, 1772-1854. Inventor. Born, and educated in Helston. He invented the rocket line apparatus which fired a rope to stricken ships. This invention went on to save at least 20,000 lives. The Life Jacket was another of his inventions. He died a pauper.

Sir Humphry Davy, 1778-1829. Chemist, Inventor, Physicist, Surgeon. Born in Penzance, he was apprenticed to an apothecary-surgeon. He moved up to London, became a Professor of Chemistry. His most famous invention, the Miner's Safety (Davy) Lamp, saved thousands of lives. He was appointed President of the Royal Society, and gave employment to Michael Faraday who was to eclipse all his deeds.

Sir Goldsworthy Gurney, 1793-1875. Architect, Inventor, Scientist, Surgeon. Born near Padstow and educated at Truro Grammar School, he was apprenticed to a Doctor of Medicine. He moved to London, and in 1832 devised the Oxy-Hydrogen Blowpipe. His other inventions included the Steam Carriage in 1825, or Horseless Carriage known as the 'Gurney Drag', and the Gurney Stove, used in various abbeys and cathedrals. The Bude Light was another invention designed for lighthouses.. Buried in Launcells churchyard.

Sir William Golding, 1911-1993. Essayist, Nobel Laureate (1983), Novelist, Playwright, Seaman, Teacher. Born in Newquay. Educated at Marlborough Grammar School and Brasenose College, Oxford. He saw active service aboard HMS Galatea in the North Atlantic and the D-Day landings. Lord of the Flies accepted for publication by Faber and Faber in 1953. Became full-time writer in 1962. Knighted in 1988.

Charles Causley, 1917-2003. Cornish Poet, Naval Coder, Playwright, Teacher. Born in Launceston, he lived much of his life in Cornwall. His verse was simple, and straightforward, and much admired by Larkin and Betjeman. Ted Hughes was his closest friend who said of him, "One of our best loved and most needed poets". Influenced by William Blake and John Clare, his poems grew out of folk songs, hymns and ballads. Awarded the Queen's Gold Medal for Poetry in 1967.

Bodmin
Shire Hall, Mount Folly,
PL31 2DQ   01208 76616
bodmintic@visit.org.uk
www.bodminlive.com

Boscastle
Boscastle Visitor Centre, The
Harbour, PL35 0HD
01840 250010
boscastlevc@btconnect.com
www.visitboscastleandtintagel.com

Bude
The Crescent Car Park,
EX23 8LE   01288 354240
bude-tic@visitbude.info
www.budelive.com

Falmouth
11 Market Strand, Prince of Wales
Pier, TR11 3DF   01326 312300
info@falmouthtic.co.uk
www.discoverfalmouth.co.uk

Fowey
Daphne Du Maurier Literary
Centre, 5 South St., PL23 1AR
01726 833616
info@fowey.co.uk
www.fowey.co.uk

Hayle
Hayle Library, Commercial Rd.,
TR27 4DE   01736 754399
hayle.library@cornwall.gov.uk

Isles of Scilly
01720 424031

Launceston
Market House, The Arcade,
PL15 8EP   01566 772321
Launcestontica@btconnect.com
www.visitlaunceston.com

Liskeard
Foresters Hall, Pike St., PL14 3JE
01579 349148
tourism@liskeard.gov.uk
www.liskeard.gov.uk

Looe
The Guildhall, Fore St., East Looe,
PL13 1AA   01503 262072
looetic@btconnect.com
www.visit-southeastcornwall.co.uk

Lostwithiel
Lostwithiel Community Centre,
Liddicoat Rd., PL22 0HE
01208 872207
tourism@lostwithieltic.wanadoo.
co.uk
www.lostwithieltic.org.uk

Mevagissey
St Georges Square, PL26 6UB
01726 844857
info@mevagissey-cornwall.co.uk
www.mevagissey-cornwall.co.uk

Newquay
Municipal Offices, Marcus Hill,
TR7 1BD   01637 854020
newquay.tic@cornwall.gov.uk
www.visitnewquay.org

Padstow
Red Brick Building, North Quay,
PL28 8AF   01841 533449
padstowtic@btconnect.com
www.padstowlive.com

Penzance
Station Approach, TR18 2NF.
01736 335530
westcornwall@nationaltrust.org.uk
www.visit-westcornwall.com

Perranporth
8 Tywarnhayle Square TR6 0ER
01872 575254
info@perranporthinfo.co.uk
www.perranporthinfo.co.uk

Redruth
The Cornwall Centre, Alma Place,
TR15 2AT   01209 219048
cornishstudies.library@cornwall.
gov.uk
www.cornwall.gov.uk

St Agnes
18 Vicarage Rd., TR5 0TL
01872 554150
ticstagnes@yahoo.co.uk
www.st-agnes.com

St Austell
By Pass Service Station, Southbourne
Rd., PL25 4RS   01726 879500
tic@cornish-riviera.co.uk
www.visitthecornishriviera.co.uk

St Ives
The Guildhall, Street an Pol,
TR26 2DS   01736 796297
stivestic@cornwall.gov.uk
www.visit-westcornwall.com

Tintagel
Tintagel Visitor Centre, Bossiney Rd.,
PL34 0NJ   01840 779084
tintagelvc@btconnect.com
www.visitboscastleandtintagel.com

Truro
Municipal Building, Boscawen St.,
TR1 2NE   01872 274555
tic@truro.gov.uk
www.truro.gov.uk

St Just
The Library, Market St.,
TR19 7HX   01736 788165
stjusttourist@cornwall.gov.uk
www.visit-westcornwall.com

St Mawes
Roseland Visitor Centre, The
Millennium Rooms, The Square,
TR2 5AG   01326 270440
manager@roselandinfo.com
www.stmawesandtheroseland.co.uk

Wadebridge
Kernow Harvest, Eddystone Rd.,
PL27 7AL   01208 816123
www.visitwadebridge.com

MAPS OF CORNWALL

█ The South East

█ The East

█ The North Coast

█ The South Coast

█ The South West

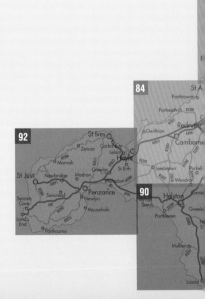

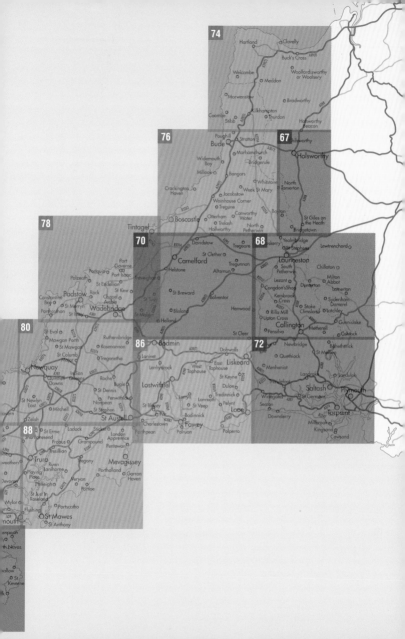

�904	Abbey/Cathedral	🍺	Pub/Inn
✕	Battle Site	🚂	Railway Interest
🏠	Bed & Breakfast Accomodation	✕🍴	Restaurant
🍵	Café	🛏	Self Catering Accommodation
🏰	Castle	🗿	Standing Stone/Barrow
⛪	Church/Chapel of Interest	🎭	Theatre/Concert Hall
🎬	Cinema	🅰	Tourist Information
⚱	Craft Interest	☼	Tumulus/Tumuli
✝	Cross	🌬	Viewpoint
🚲	Cycleway	✕	Windmill/Wind Farm
🎡	Fun Park/Leisure Park	⊕	Airfield
☀	Hill Fort/Ancient Settlement	◢	Aquarium
🏛	Historic Building	🚤	Boat Trips
🏨	Hotel	⛺	Camping Site (Tents)
🏭	Industrial Interest	🚐	Caravan Site
🏎	Karting	👫	Ferry (Pedestrians)
🗼	Lighthouse	🚗	Ferry (Vehicles)
⛏	Mining Interest/Engine Houses	🎣	Fishing Trips
☆	Miscellaneous/Natural Attraction	⛳	9/18 Hole Golf Course
🏛	Museum/Art Gallery	⚓	Harbour
🏺	Pottery	🛟	Inshore Rescue Boat

🅖	Leisure/Sports Centre
🚣	Lifeboat
🅿	Parking
🍴	Picnic Site
⛺🚐	Tents & Caravans
⛵	Sailing
🏄	Surfing
🅰	Tourist Information
🏄	Windsurfing
▾	Youth Hostel
🚜	Agricultural Interest
🌳	Arboretum
🐦	Bird Reserve
🌸	Garden of Interest
🍇	Vineyard
🚶	Walks/Nature Trails
✦	Wildlife Park
🐾	Zoo
🅿	National Trust Car Park

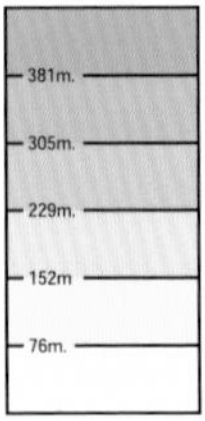

381m.	
305m.	
229m.	
152m	
76m.	

▬▬▬▬	A Road
▬▬▬▬	B Road
·········	Minor Road
- - - - -	Other Road or Track (not necessarily with public or vehicular access)
●─────	Railway
············	Cycleway

Open Space owned by the National Trust

Built-up Area

Scale 1:100,000

0	1	(miles) 2
0	1	2 (km)

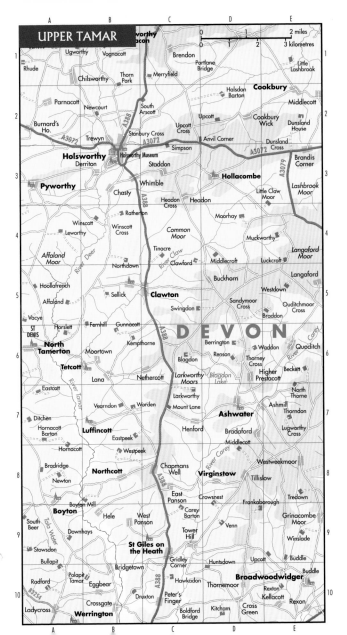

UPPER TAMAR

worthy
acon

A3072

A3088

DEVON

River Deer

River Claw

River Tamar

River Carey

River Carey

Tala Water

A3079

A3254

Ugworthy
Rhude
Vognacott
Brendon
Portlane
Bridge
Little
Lashbrook
Chilsworthy
Thorn
Park
Merryfield
Halsdon
Barton
Cookbury
Parnacott
Newcourt
South
Arscott
Upcott
Cookbury
Wick
Middlecott
Burnard's
Ho.
Trewyn
Upcott
Cross
Anvil Corner
Dunsland
House
Holsworthy
Derriton
Stanbury Cross
Holsworthy Museum
Simpson
Dunsland
Cross
Brandis
Corner
Pyworthy
Whimble
Staddon
Hollacombe
Lashbrook
Moor
Chasty
Headon
Cross
Headon
Little Claw
Moor
Ratherton
Moorhay
Winscott
Leworthy
Winscott
Cross
Common
Moor
Muckworthy
Langaford
Moor
Affaland
Moor
Northdown
Tinacre
Clawford
Middlecroft
Luckcroft
Langaford
Hoollafrench
Sellick
Buckhorn
Westdown
Affaland
Clawton
Sandymoor
Cross
Ouditchmoor
Cross
Vacye
Horslett
Fernhill
Gunnacott
Swingdon
Braddon
ST
DENIS
North
Tamerton
Moortown
Kempthorne
Berrington
Waddon
Quoditch
Tetcott
Lana
Nethercott
Blagdon
Renson
Thorney
Cross
Higher
Prestacott
Beckett
Eastcott
Larkworthy
Moors
Blagdon
Lake
North
Thorne
Ditchen
Hornacott
Barton
Vearndon
Worden
Larkworthy
Mount Lane
Ashwater
Ashmill
Thorndon
Hornacott
Luffincott
Eastpeek
Henford
Bradaford
Lugworthy
Cross
Bradridge
Newton
Westpeek
Middlecott
Westweekmoor
Northcott
Chapmans
Well
Virginstow
Tillislow
Tredown
Boyton Mill
Hele
West
Panson
East
Panson
Crowsnest
Frankaborough
Grinacombe
Moor
Boyton
South
Beer
Downhays
Carey
Barton
Venn
Winslade
Stowsdon
Tower
Hill
Upcott
Buddle
Bullapit
St Giles on
the Heath
Gridley
Corner
Huntsdown
Broadwoodwidger
Buddle
Radford
Polapit
Tamar
Eggbear
Bridgetown
Hawkadon
Thornemoor
Rexton
Kellacott
Rexon
Ladycross
Crossgate
Werrington
Druxton
Peter's
Finger
Boldford
Bridge
Kitcham
Cross
Green

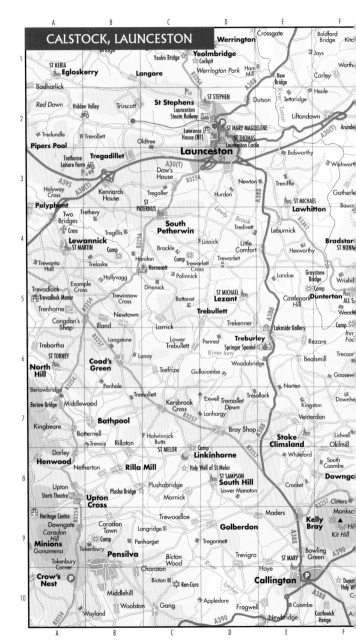

CALSTOCK, LAUNCESTON

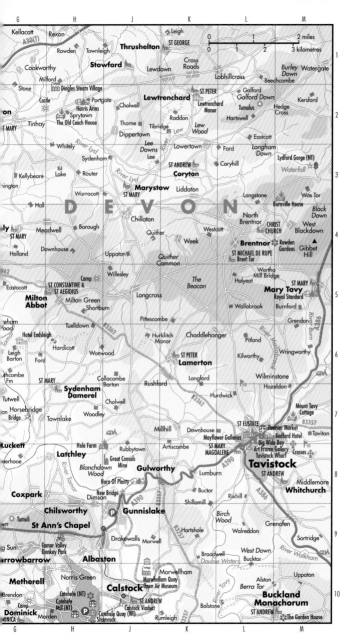

Grid columns: G H J K L M
Grid rows: 1 2 3 4 5 6 7 8 9 10

Kellacott
A30(T)
Rexon
Leigh
ST GEORGE
Rowden
Townleigh
Thrushelton
Cross
Roads
Cookworthy
Stowford
Lewdown
Lobhillcross
Burley
Down
Watergate
Milford
Beechcombe
Stone
Dingles Steam Village
Portgate
ST PETER
Galford
Galford Down
Castle
Lewtrenchard
Lewtrenchard
Manor
Kersford
on
Harris Arms
Cholwell
Tumulus
Hedge
Cross
T MARY
Tinhay
Sprytown
The Old Coach House
Thorne
Tibridge
Raddon
Lew
Wood
Hartswell
Eastcott
Dippertown
River Lyd
Whitely
Lee
Downs
Lowertown
Ford
Longham
Down
Lydford Gorge (NT)
Sydenham
Lee
Waterfall
Kellybeare
Lake
Router
River Lyd
ST ANDREW
Coryton
Coryhill
mington
Marystow
ST MARY
Liddaton
Langstone
Was Tor
Hall
Warracott
D E V O N
Burnville House
Black
Down
Chillaton
North
Brentor
West
Blackdown
ly
ST MARY
Meadwell
Borough
Quither
Westcott
CHRIST
CHURCH
Week
Brentor
Rowden
Gardens
Gibbet
Hill
Holland
Downhouse
Uppaton
Quither
Common
ST MICHAEL DE RUPE
Brent Tor
Wortha
Mill Bridge
ST MARY
462
Camp
Willesley
The
Beacon
Holyeat
Mary Tavy
Royal Standard
Eastacott
ST CONSTANTINE &
ST AEGIDIUS
**Milton
Abbot**
Milton Green
Shortburn
Longcross
Wallabrook
Burnford
eham
ood
Tuelldown
B3362
Pittescombe
Grendon
River Mallabrook
Hotel Endsleigh
Hurlditch
Manor
Chaddlehanger
Pitland
Wringworthy
Leigh
Barton
Hardicott
Wonwood
ST PETER
Lamerton
Kilworthy
thcombe
Fm
ST MARY
Collacombe
Barton
Rushford
Langford
Wilminstone
Tutwell
**Sydenham
Damerel**
Cholwell
Hurdwick
Hazeldon
on
Bridge
Horsebridge
Townlake
Woodley
Mount Tavy
Cottage
B3357
Luckett
Latchley
Hele Farm
Millhill
Downhouse
Mayflower Galleries
Artiscombe
ST EUSTACE
Pannier Market
Bedford Hotel
Taviton
erhoe
Rubbytown
ST MARY
MAGDALENE
Big Wide Bay
Art Frame Gallery
Tavistock Wharf
Blanchdown
Wood
Great Consols
Mine
Gulworthy
Lumburn
Tavistock
ST ANDREW
Middlemore
Whitchurch
Coxpark
Horn Of Plenty
Buctor
Rixhill
A386
New Bridge
Dimson
Shillamill
Chilsworthy
Gunnislake
A390
B3357
Birch
Wood
Walreddon
Grenofen
St Ann's Chapel
Drakewalls
Morwell
Hartshole
West Down
Bucktor
Sortridge
g Sun
Tamar Valley
Donkey Park
Broadwell
Double Waters
River Walkham
rrowbarrow
Albaston
Uppaton
Morwellham
Alston
Berra Tor
**Buckland
Monachorum**
Metherell
Norris Green
Morwellham Quay
Open Air Museum
Brendon
Camp
Cotehele (NT)
Calstock
ST ANDREW
Balstone
ST ANDREW
DOMINICK
MINICA
Cotehele
Mill (NT)
Morden
ST ANDREW
Calstock Viaduct
Cotehele Quay (NT)
Shamrock
Rumleigh
The Garden House
B3357

0 ___ 1 ___ 2 miles
0 1 2 3 kilometres

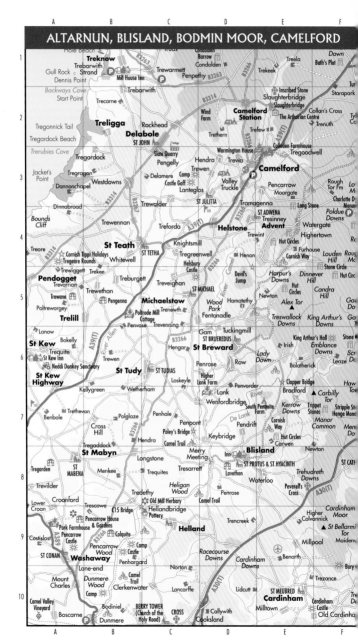

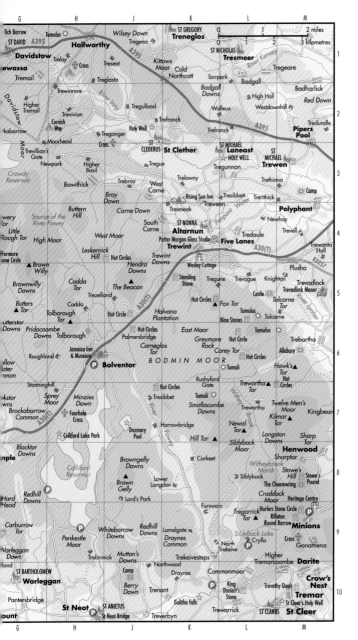

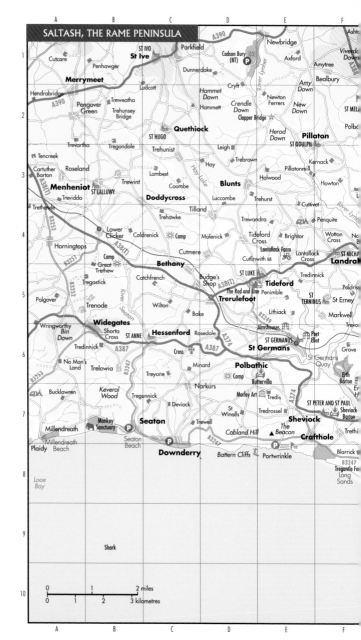

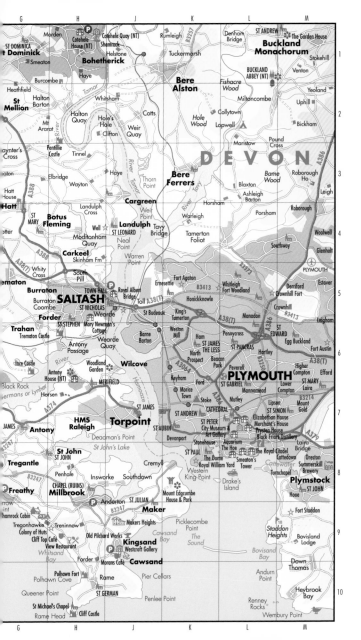

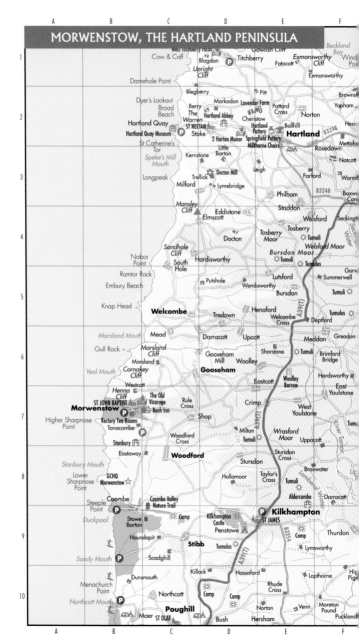

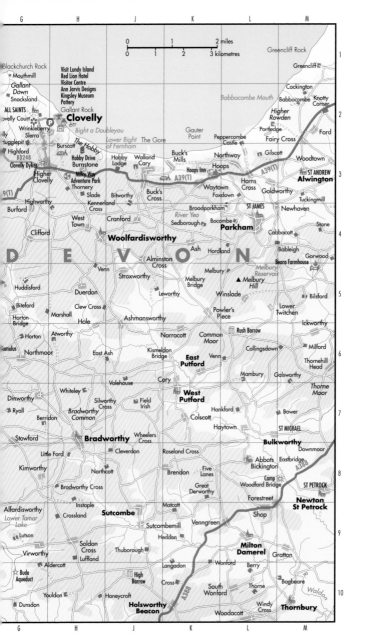

0   1   2 miles
0   1   2   3 kilometres

Greencliff Rock

1

Blackchurch Rock
Mouthmill
Gallant Down
Snacksland
ALL SAINTS
Clovelly Court
Wrinkleberry
Sierra
Jugglepit
Highford
Clovelly Dykes
B3248
Higher Clovelly
A9(T)
Highworthy
Burford

Greencliff

Cockington
Babbacombe Mouth
Babbacombe
Knotty Corner

Higher Rowden

Visit Lundy Island
Red Lion Hotel
Visitor Centre
Ann Jarvis Designs
Kingsley Museum
Pottery
Gallant Rock

Clovelly

Bight a Doubleyou
The Hobby
Burscott
Hobby Drive
Burnstone
Hobby Lodge
Milky Way
Adventure Park
Thornery
Slade
Kennerland Cross

Lower Bight of Fernham
The Gore

Walland Cary

Gauter Point
Peppercombe Castle
Portledge
Fairy Cross
Ford

Buck's Mills
Northway
Hoops Inn
Hoops

ST ANDREW
Alwington

Woodtown

Horns Cross
Goldworthy
Tuckingmill

Bihworthy
Buck's Cross

Waytown
Foxdown

Newhaven

2

3

Broadparkham
Sedborough
Bocombe

ST JAMES
Parkham

Cabbacott
Stone

West Town
Cranford
River Yeo

Woolfardisworthy

Bableigh
Gorwood

Clifford

Ash
Hordland

Beara Farmhouse

D E V O N

Alminston Cross

Melbury Reservoir

Huddisford

Verin
Stroxworthy

Melbury
Melbury Bridge
▲ *Melbury Hill*

Bilsford

Biteford
Horton Bridge
Horton

Duerdon
Clew Cross
Hole

Leworthy

Winslade

Lower Twitchen

Marshall

Ashmansworthy

Powler's Piece

Ickworthy

4

5

Cumulus
Northmoor
Atworthy

East Ash

Narracott
Kismeldon Bridge

Common Moor
Rush Barrow

Venn
East Putford

Collingsdown

Milford

Thornehill Head

6

Dinworthy
Whiteley

Volehouse

Cory

Mambury
Galsworthy

Thorne Moor

Ryall
Berridon

Silworthy Cross
Bradworthy Common
Field Irish

West Putford

Hankford
Colscott
Haytown

Bower

7

Stowford
Little Ford

Bradworthy
Wheelers Cross

Cleverdon
Roseland Cross

ST MICHAEL
Bulkworthy
Downmoor

A388

Kimworthy

Northcott

Brendon
Five Lanes

Abbots Bickington
Eastbridge

8

Bradworthy Cross

Great Derworthy
Camp
Woodford Bridge

ST PETROCK

Alfardisworthy
Lower Tamar Lake

Instaple
Crossland

Sutcombe

Matcott

Forestreet

Newton St Petrock

9

Lutson

Virworthy

Soldon Cross
Luffland

Thuborough

Sutcombemill
Heddon

Venngreen
Shop

Milton Damerel
Gratton

Aldercott

High Barrow

Langadon
Wonford
Berry

Bagbeare

Waldon

10

Bude Aqueduct

Youldon

Honeychurch

Cross

South Wonford

Thorne

Windy Cross

Thornbury

Dunsdon

Holsworthy Beacon

Woodacott

0 1 2 miles
0 1 2 3 kilometres

Widemo
Sand
Wanson Mou
Foxhole Point
Millook Haven
Outdoor Adventure
Cancleave Strand
Millo
Dizzard Point
Millook
Common
Chipman Strand
Treborfoot
Cornish
Way
Dizzard

Tresmorn
Trengayor
Pencannow
Point
St Gennys
Trewint
ST GENESIUS
Bray's Point
Camp
Treworgie
Cambeak
Crackington
Coxford
Trencres
Haven

Little Strand
Rosecare
Hallagather
The Strangles
Crackington
Wainhouse
The
Trevigue
Corner
Beac
Voter Run
Baypark
Trevigue Wildlife Conservation
Rosecure
Rusey Beach
High
Pengold
Pencuke
Villa
Cliff
Round
Buckator
Camp
Hayes
Newton
Tresparrett
Tumuli
Gull Rock
Posts
B3263
Trengune
Beeny Sisters
Camp
Collamoor
Fire Deacon Point
Ringford
Tresparrett
Cansford
Head
Downs
Trevillian
Pentargon
Beeny
Trebyla
B3263
Cocksport
Pencarrol
Marshgate
Cornish
Penally Point (NT)
Museum of Witchcraft
Tresparrett
Way
Wilapark (NT)
ST JULIOT'S
Cardew
Short
The Old Parsonage
Hennett
ST DENIS
Long Island
Napoleon Inn
Valency
Trevilla
Mill
Island
Boscastle
Bottreaux
Valley (NT)
The Old Rectory
Otterham
Roose
ST SYMPHORIAN'S Castle
Treworld
R. Valency
Otterham
Trelash
Trevalga
MINSTER
Lesnewth
Trevilla
Down
Cross
ST PETROCK
ST MICHAEL
Helset
Down
Hallgarden
Polrunny
Tredorne
Tregrylls
Trethevey
Copplestone
Otterham
Tregray
St Nectan's Glen
Reddivallen
Station
Halgabron
Waterfall & Chapel
Vendown
Hallwell
Tumuli
Tumuli
St Nectan's
Waterpit
Cross
Hendra
Hallworthy
Trenale
Kieve
Down
Hendraburnick
Tich Barrow
Tumulus

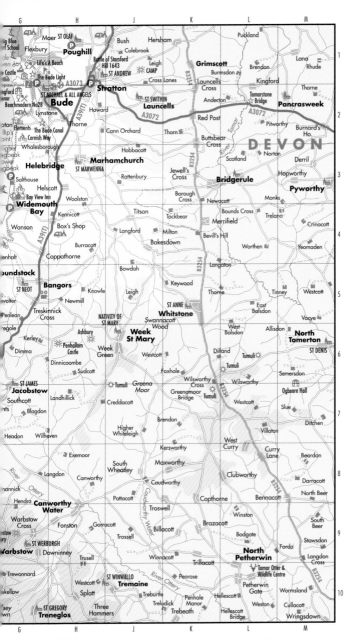

G H J K L M

Long Island

1

The Sisters   Lye
Willapark   Rock

Barras Nose
Tintagel Castle
Tintagel   The Old Post Office (NT)   Bossiney   St Nectan's Glen
King Arthur's Great Halls   Tintagel Castle
Visitor Centre   The Island   Halgabron

Tintagel Head   Trethevey

ST MATERIANA   Tintagel
Dunderhole Point   Glebe   Treven   Trenale
Cliff   Tregatta

Hole Beach   Truas

2

Treknow   Trewarmett
Trebarwith   B3263
Gull Rock   Strand
Dennis Point   Mill House Inn
Backways Cove   Trebarwith

Start Point   Trecarne

3

Tregonnick Tail   Treligga   Rockhead

Tregardock Beach   Delabole
Trerubies Cove   ST JOHN

Tregardock   Slate Quarry
Pengelly

Jacket's Point   Tregagon   Delamere

Westdowns

4

PORT ISAAC   Dannonchapel
The Edge   Port Isaac Bay   Trewalder
The Old School Hotel   Delabole Point
The Slipway Hotel   Ranie Point   Trewennan
Kellan   Varley Head   Dinnabroad
Head   Scarnor
Point   Tresungers   Bounds Cliff
Point
yden   ST PETER   Knightsmill
oint   Port Isaac   Roscarrock   St Teath   ST TETHA
Portquin   Cellars   Port Gaverne   Whitewell   Tregrennwell

5

Porteath Barn   Longcross   Cross Shaft   Trewetha   Treore   Tregeare Rounds   Trekee
Bee Centre   Victorian   Trefreock   Pendogget   Trewigget   Cornish Tippi Holidays   Treburgett   Treveighan
Porteath   Garden   Trelights   Tresungers   Trevorrian   Trewethan
Mesmear   Wave 7 Studio

ST ENDELLIENTA   Treharrock   Trewane
Plain Street   St Endellion   Poltrewan   Pengenna
Gunvenna   Trevathan Farm   Pennytinney   Trelill
Trevathan   Trentinney   Lanow   Penvose   Poltrode Mill
anger   St Minver   Tregellist   Bokelly   Cottage

6

7

rizzick   Tregwarmond   Trewethern   St JAMES   Trequite   Trewen
Trevine   St Kew Inn   St Tudy   ST TUDIAS
Blakes   Rooke   St Kew   Neddi
Keiro   Tredower   Malsters   Pellengarrow   Donkey Sanctuary   Kellygreen   Wetherham
Old Windmill   Arms   Chapel   St Kew
ilver   Lower   Amble   Highway
Dinham   Amble   Tregorden   Benbole   Trethevan   Palglaze   Penhale

8

9

Trewornan   Kelly   Cross
Tregunna   Castle Killibury   Hill   Tregaddock   Hendra
ean   Burniere   Three Holes   Tregarden   St Mabyn   Longstone
Camel Trail   Bodieve   Cross   ST   Trequites
Trevanson   Tregunna   Tredethy   Old Mill Herbary
C15 Bridge   MABENA   Trevilder   Croanford   Trescowe   Pottery
itecross   Chase Art Gallery   Trenant   Egloshayle   Lower   Pencarrow House   Hellandbridge
St Breock   Tristan's Grave   ST CONAN   Clapper   Croan   & Gardens
Royal Cornwall   Wadebridge   Sladesbridge   C15 Bridge   Helland
Showground   ST BREOCK   Eglos Pottery
Inscribed   Polmorla   Treneague   Trewen   Pendavey   Wood Design   Park
Stone   Nanscow   Tredannick

10

G H J K L M

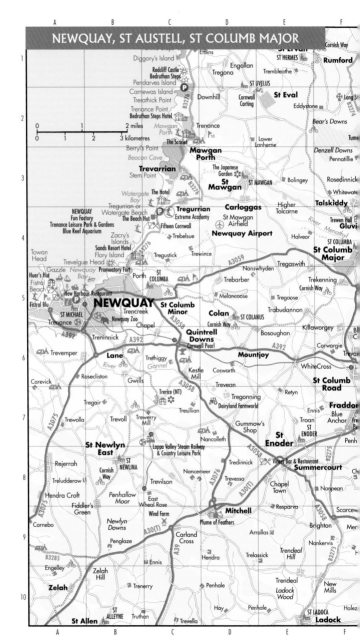

St Evan
Cornish Way
 St Hermes
Rumford

Diggory's Steps
Ethins
Engollan
Trembleathe

Redcliff Castle
Bedruthan Steps
Pendarves Island
Downhill
ST UVELUS
St Eval
Eddystone
Long S

Carnewas Island
Tretathick Point
Trenance Point
Bedruthan Steps Hotel
Cornwall
Carting
Bear's Downs
Tume

0   1   2 miles
0   1   2   3 kilometres
Mawgan Porth
Trenance
Lower Lanherne
Denzell Downs
Pennatillie

Berry's Point
Beacon Cove
The Scarlet
Mawgan Porth
The Japanese Garden
Rosedinnick
Whitewate

Trevarrian
Stem Point
St Mawgan
ST MAWGAN
Bolingey
Talskiddy

Watergate Bay
The Hotel
Tregurrian or Watergate Beach
Carloggas
Higher Tolcarne
River Menathyl
Trewen Hall
Gluvi

NEWQUAY
Fun Factory
Trenance Leisure Park & Gardens
Blue Reef Aquarium
The Beach Hut
Tregurrian
Extreme Academy
St Mawgan Airfield
Fifteen Cornwall
ST COLUMBA
St Columb Major

Zacry's Islands
Flory Island
Sands Resort Hotel
Trebelsue
Newquay Airport
Halveor

Towan Head
Trevelgue Head
Tregustick
Trewince
Tregaswith

Gazzle
Newquay Bay
Promontory Fort
Porth
ST COLUMBA
Nanswhyden
Trebarber
Trekenning
Cornish Way

Huer's Hut
Fistral Beach
New Harbour Restaurant
Trencreek
Melancoose
Tregoose
Trabudannon

Fistral Blu
ST MICHAEL
Newquay Zoo
NEWQUAY
St Columb Minor
Colan
ST COLANUS
Bosoughan
Killaworgey
B
C

Trenance
Chapel
Quintrell Downs
Cornish Way

Trevemper
Treninnick
Lane
Trethiggy
Cornwall Pearl
Mountjoy
WhiteCross
Trevan
Corwgie

Carevick
Rasecliston
Gwills
Kestle Mill
Cosworth
Trevean
Retyn
St Columb Road

Tregair
Trerice (NT)
Tregonning
Dairyland Farmworld
Ennis
Fraddor
Blue Anchor
Fr

Trewolla
Trevoll
Trewerry Mill
Tresillian
Gummow's Shop
Nancolleth
Troan
ST ENODER
Penh

St Newlyn East
Lappa Valley Steam Railway & Country Leisure Park
St Enoder
Vines Bar & Restaurant
Summercourt
Chi

Rejerrah
ST NEWLINA
Cornish Way
Nancemeer
Tredinnick
Trevessa
Chapel Town
Resparva
Nanpean

Treludderow
Penhallow Moor
Trevilson
ST A30(T)
Scarcew

Hendra Croft
Fiddler's Green
East Wheal Rose
Wind Farm
Mitchell
Plume of Feathers
Arrallas
Brighton
Mer

Carnebo
Newlyn Downs
Penglaze
A30(T)
Carland Cross
Hendra
Trelassick
Trendeal Hill
Nankervis
H

Engelley
B3285
Ennis
A39
Penhale
Trendeal Ladock Wood
New Mills

Zelah
Zelah Hill
Trenerry
Hay
Penhale
ST LADOCA
Haldez
Ladock

St Allen
ST ALLEYNE
Truthan
Trevella

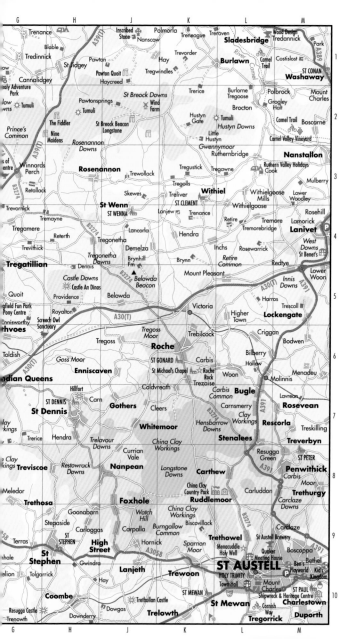

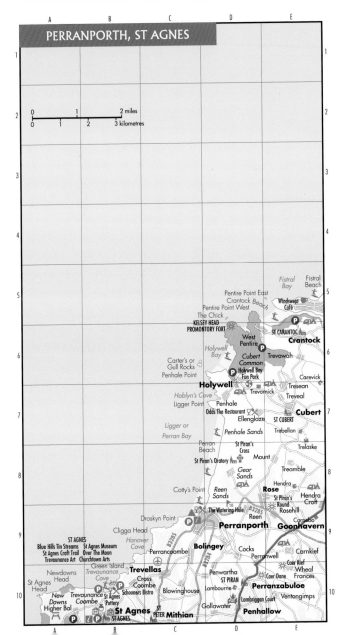

Fistral Bay
Fistral Beach

Pentire Point East
Crantock Beach
Pentire Point West
The Chick
KELSEY HEAD
PROMONTORY FORT
Windswept Café
ST CARANTOC
Crantock

West Pentire
Cubert Common
Trevowah

Holywell Bay
Holywell Bay Fun Park
Carter's or Gull Rocks
Penhale Point
Holywell
Trevornick
Carevick
Tresean
Treveal

Hoblyn's Cove
Ligger Point
Penhale
Odds The Restaurant
Ellenglaze
ST CUBERT
Treval
Cubert
Trebellan

Ligger or Perran Bay
Penhale Sands
Trelaske

Perran Beach
St Piran's Cross
St Piran's Oratory
Mount
Treamble

Gear Sands
Hendra
Rose
St Piran's Round
Rosehill
Hendra Croft

Cotty's Point
Reen Sands
Reen
Carnebo
Goonhavern

Droskyn Point
The Watering Hole
Perranporth

Cligga Head
Hanover Cove
Bolingey
Cocks
Perranwell
Carnkief

ST AGNES
Blue Hills Tin Streams
St Agnes Craft Trail
Trevaunance Art
St Agnes Museum
Over The Moon
Churchtown Arts
Perrancoombe
Caer Kief
Wheal Frances

Green Island
Trevaunance Cove
Trevellas
Penwartha
ST PIRAN
Caer Dane
Perranzabuloe
Ventongimps

Newdowns Head
St Agnes Head
New Downs
Higher Bal
Trevaunance Coombe
St Agnes Pottery
Cross Coombe
Schooners Bistro
Blowinghouse
Lambourne
Lambriggan Court
Gollawater
Penhallow

St Agnes
ST AGNES
ST PETER Mithian

83

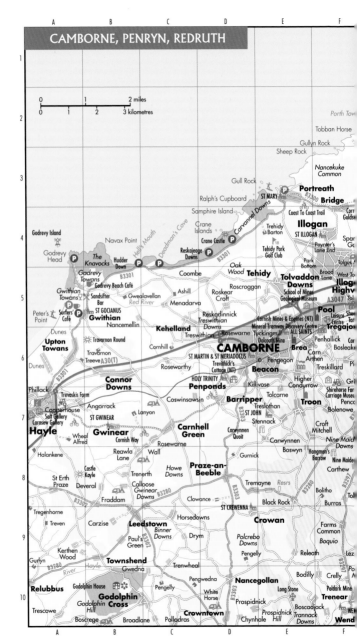

0   1   2 miles
0   1   2   3 kilometres

Porth Tow

Tobban Horse

Gullyn Rock

Sheep Rock

Nancekuke Common

Gull Rock

Ralph's Cupboard

Portreath

ST MARY

Bridge

Coast To Coast Trail

Samphire Island

Carvannel Downs

Cor
Golds

Crane Islands

Deadman's Cove

Trehidy Barton

Illogan

ST ILLOGAN

Spar
Go

Godrevy Island

Navax Point

Hell's Mouth

Crane Castle

Reskajeage Downs

Oak Wood

Tehidy Park Golf Club

Park Bottom

Paynter's Lane End

Tolgus

Godrevy Head

The Knavocks

Hudder Down

Godrevy Towans

Godrevy Beach Café

Coombe

Tehidy

Roscroggan

Tolvaddon Downs

School of Mines
Geological Museum

Broad Lane

West To

**Illog
Highv**

A3047

Tol

Gwithian Towans

Sandsifter Bar

Gwealavellan

Red River

Ashill

Roskear Croft

Menadarva

Reskadinnick

Pool

Leisure
Centre

Shee
Tar

Peter's Point

Surfers' Café

ST GOCIANUS

Gwithian

Nancemellin

Treswithian
Downs

Treswithian

Cornish Mines & Engines (NT)
Mineral Tramway Discovery Centre
Tuckingmill   ALL SAINTS

Tregajo

Dunes

Upton Towans

Travarnon Round

Kehelland

Rosewarne

Dolcoath Mine

Penhallick

Car
Bosleake

Cornhill

CAMBORNE

Brea

Carn
Arthen

Dunes

Travarnon

Treeve A30(T)

Roseworthy

ST MARTIN & ST MERIADOCUS

Trevithick's
Cottage (NT)

Pengegon

Carn
Arthen

Treskillard

Phillack

Connor Downs

Penponds

HOLY TRINITY

Beacon

Killivose

Higher
Condurrow

Gri

Shirehorse Far
Carriage Muse

Trevaskis Farm

Angarrack

Coswinsawsin

Barripper

Tolcarne

Troon

Penco
Bolenowe

Copperhouse

Salt Gallery

Carnsew Gallery

Lanyon

ST GWINEAR

Treslothan

ST JOHN

Croft
Mitchell

Hayle

Wheal Alfred

Gwinear

Cornish Way

Carnhell Green

Stennack

Carwynnen
Quoit

Nine Maid
Downs

Rosewarne

Carwynnen

Boswyn

Hangman's
Barrow

Nine Maide

Halankene

Reawla Lane

Wall

Praze-an-Beeble

Howe Downs

Gurnick

Carthew

St Erth
Praze

Castle
Kayle

Deveral

Trenerth

Calloose
Gwinear
Downs

Tremayne

Resrs

Bolitho

Tol

Fraddam

Clowance

ST CREWENNA

Black Rock

Burras

Tregenhorne

Horsedowns

Crowan

Farms
Common

Treven

Carzise

Leedstown

Binner
Downs

Drym

Polcrebo
Downs

Boquio

Kerthen
Wood

Paul's
Green

Pengelly

Releath

Lez

Gurlyn

B3280

Hayle
River

Townshend

Gwedna

Trenwheal

Pengwedna

Bodilly

Crelly

Nancegollan

Long Stone

Poldark Mine

Relubbus

Godolphin House

Pengelly

White
Horse

Prospidnick

Trenear

Trescowe

Godolphin
Hill

**Godolphin
Cross**

Prospidnick
Hill

Boscadjack

Trannack
Downs

WE

Boscrege

Broadlane

Polladras

Crowntown

Chynhale

Wend

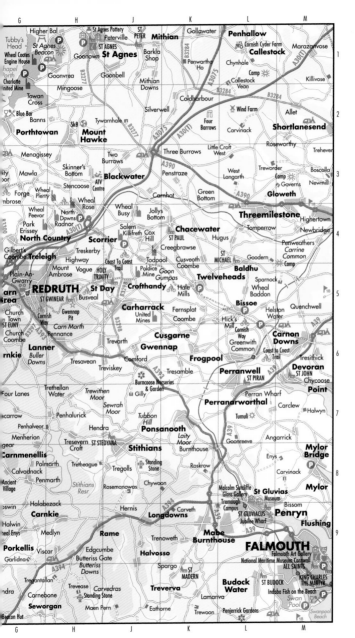

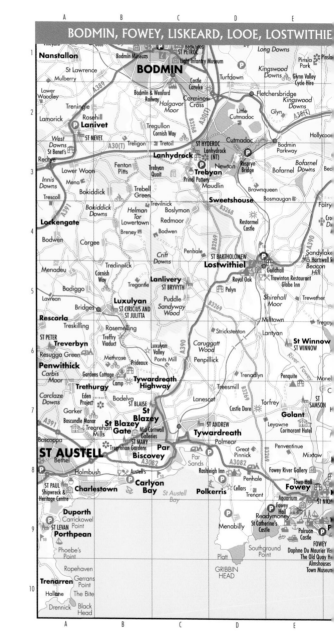

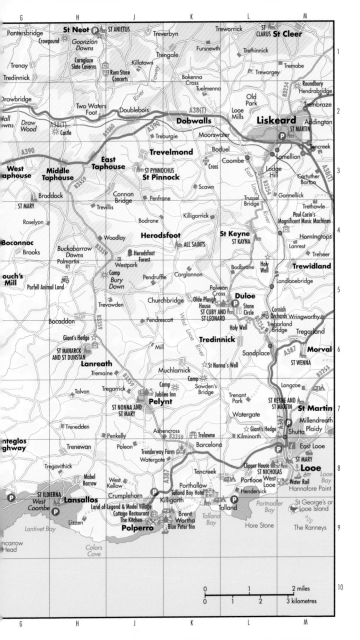

Row 1:
Pantersbridge, St Neot, ST ANIETUS, Treverbyn, Treworrick, ST CLARUS, St Cleer, Crowpound, Goonzion Downs, Fursnewth, Trefhinnick, Tremabe, Trengale, Killatown, Bokenna Cross, Tuelmenna, Treworgey, Trembraze, Trenay, Carnglaze Slate Caverns, Rum Store Concerts, River Fowey

Row 2:
Drawbridge, Two Waters Foot, Doublebois, A38(T), Old Park, Roundbury, Hendrabridge, Draw Wood, Castle, Dobwalls, Looe Mills, Liskeard, Addington, ST MARTIN, Moorswater, Lamellion, Treburgie, Tencreek

Row 3:
West aphouse, Middle Taphouse, East Taphouse, Trevelmond, ST PYNNOCHUS, St Pinnock, Boduel, Coombe, Lodge Hill, Certuther Barton, Braddock, ST MARY, Connon Bridge, Penfrane, Cross, Scawn, Trussel Bridge, Gormellick, Trevillis, Treree, Trethawle

Row 4:
Roselyon, Bodrane, Killigorrick, St Keyne, ST KAYNA, Paul Corin's Magnificent Music Machines, Horningtops, Boconnoc, Brooks, Woodlay, Herodsfoot, ALL SAINTS, Lanrest, Treheer, Buckabarrow Downs, Polmartin, Herodsfoot Forest, Bodbrane, Holy Well, Trewidland

Row 5:
ouch's Mill, Porfell Animal Land, Westpark, Camp Bury Down, Pendruffle, Carglannon, Polvean Cross, Landlooebridge, Trevawden, Churchbridge, Olde Plough House, ST CUBY AND ST LEONARD, Duloe, Stone Circle, Cornish Orchards, Wringworthy, Bocaddon, Pendrescott, Holy Well, Tregarland Bridge, Tregarland

Row 6:
Giant's Hedge, ST MANARCK AND ST DUNSTAN, Mill, Tredinnick, Sandplace, Morval, ST WENNA, Lanreath, Tremaine, Muchlarnick, St Nonna's Well

Row 7:
Talvan, Tregarrick, Camp Jubilee Inn, Pelynt, ST NONNA ST MARY, Camp Sowden's Bridge, Trenant Park, ST KEYNE AND ST MARTIN, St Martin, Longcoe, Millendreath, Plaidy, Trenedden, Watergate, Shutta

Row 8:
nteglos ghway, Trenewan, Penkelly, Poleon, Trenderway Farm, Watergate, Ashencross, ST NONNA, Trelawne, Barcelona, Giant's Hedge, Kilminorth, East Looe, ST MARY, Looe, Tregavithick, Mabel Barrow, West Kellow, Crumplehorn, Tencreek, Porthallow, Talland Bay Hotel, Clipper House, ST NICHOLAS, Portlooe, West Looe, Hendersick, Water Rail, Hannafore Point

Row 9:
ST ILDIERNA, West Coombe, Lansallos, Lizzen, Land & Model Village, Cottage Restaurant, The Kitchen, Polperro, Killigarth, Brent Wortha, Blue Peter Inn, Talland, Portnadler Bay, St George's or Looe Island, Hore Stone, The Ranneys, Looe Bay, Lantivet Bay, Colors Cove

Row 10:
ncarrow Head

Scale:
0 — 1 — 2 miles
0 — 1 — 2 — 3 kilometres

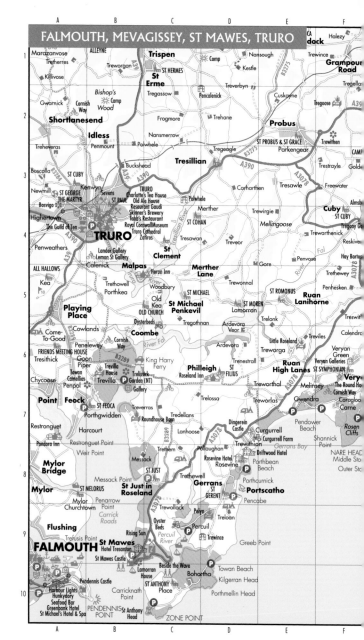

Marazanvose
Tretherres
Killivose
Gwarnick

ALLEYNE
Treworgan
Bishop's
Camp Wood
Cornish Way

Trispen
ST HERMES
St Erme
Tregassow
Frogmore
Nansmerrow
Polwhele

Camp
Kestle
Nansough
Treverbyn
Pencalenick
Trehane

Grampour Road
Tregella
Cuskayne
Trewithen

Tregoose
CAMP

Shortlanesend
Idless
Penmount

Probus
ST PROBUS & ST GRACE
Parkengear

Treheveras
Boscolla
Newmill
Bosvigo
Highertown
Penweathers

ST CUBY
ST GEORGE THE MARTYR
Kenwyn
Sevens
ST PAUL
TRURO
Charlotte's Tea House
Old Ale House
Restaurant Gaudi
Skinner's Brewery
Tabb's Restaurant
Royal Cornwall Museum
Truro Cathedral
Zafiros
The Guild of Ten

Buckshead
Tresillian
Polwhele
Merther
ST COHAN
Tresawan
Trevor

Carharthen
Trewirgie
Mellingoose
Gore

Tresawle
Trewarthenick
Penvose

Cuby
ST CUBY
Tregony Ge
Reskive
Hay Barton
Trethewey
Penhesken

TRURO
Lander Gallery
Leman St Gallery
Calenick
Malpas
Heron Inn

St Clement
Merther Lane
Woodbury
ST MICHAEL
Trewonnal

ALL HALLOWS
Kea
Trethowell
Porthkea
Old Kea
OLD CHURCH

ST ROMONUS
Ruan Lanihorne

Playing Place
Come-To-Good
Cowlands
Penelewey
FRIENDS MEETING HOUSE
Tresithick
Chycoose
Coombe
Oysterbeds
River Fal

St Michael Penkevil
Tregothnan
Ardevora Veor
Ardevora

ST MOREN
Lamorran
Trelonk
Little Roseland
Treworga

Treswit
Calendra
Treviles
Veryan Green
Veryan Galleries

Point
Feock
Goon Piper
Iawan
Camellias
Penpol
Trevilla
Trellissick Garden (NT)
Gallery
King Harry Ferry
ST FILIUS
Roseland Inn
Philleigh
Trelossa
Trenestrall
Treworthal

Ruan High Lanes
ST SYMPHONIAN
Melinsey
Treworlas
Gwendra

Very
The Round Ho
Cornish Way
Caragloo
Carne

Restronguet
Pandora Inn
Harcourt
Restronguet Point
Weir Point
ST FEOCA
Porthgwidden
Treverras
Roundhouse Barn
Tredellans
Lanhoose

Dingerein Castle
Curgurrell
Trewithian

Pendower Beach
Shannick Point

Rosen Cliffs

NARE HEAD
Middle Sto
Outer Sto

Mylor Bridge
Mylor
ST MELORUS
Mylor Churchtown
Penarrow Point
Carrick Roads
Messack
Messack Point
ST JUST
Trethewell

St Just in Roseland
Pollaughan
Rosevine Hotel
Rosevine
Gerrans
ST GERENT
Driffwood Hotel
Porthbean Beach
Porthcurnick
Portscatho
Pencabe

Flushing
Trefusis Point
FALMOUTH
Rising Sun
St Mawes
Hotel Tresanton
St Mawes Castle

Lamorran House
Trewollack
Oyster Beds
Percuil River
Percuil
Pelyn
Treloan

Trewince
Greeb Point

Harbour Lights
Hunkydory
Seafood Bar
Greenbank Hotel
St Michael's Hotel & Spa
Pendennis Castle
PENDENNIS POINT
Carricknath Point
Beside the Wave
Lamorran House
ST ANTHONY Place
Bohortha
St Anthony Head
ZONE POINT
Towan Beach
Kilgerran Head
Porthmellin Head

89

THE LIZARD PENINSULA

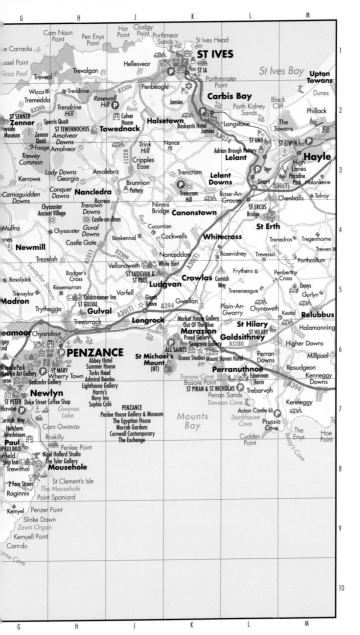

CALENDAR OF EVENTS

January
Wadebridge. North Cornwall Point to Point

February
St Columb. Cornish Hurling
St Ives Hurling the Silver Ball

March
Cotehele Daffodils Festival
Eden Bulb Mania
Liskeard Annual Art Exhibition
Mount Edgcumbe Camelia Collection
St Piran's Day

April
Boscastle Walking Week
Camborne Trevithick Day
St Endellion Music Festival

May
Cornish International Male Voice Choir Festival
Falmouth Asparagus Festival
Fowey Daphne Du Maurier Festival of Arts & Literature
Helston Furry/Flora Dance
Launceston Steam & Vintage Rally
Newquay Longboard Championships
Padstow 'Obby Oss' Celebrations

June
Falmouth. Fal River Festival
Kernow Midsummer Bonfires
Liskeard Festival
Mevagissey Festival Week
Penzance. Golowan Festival
Polperro Festival
Saltash Town Regatta
St Keverne. An Gov Day
St Merryn Steam Rally
Wadebridge. Royal Cornwall Show

July
Boconnoc Steam Fair
Bodmin Riding & Heritage Day
InterCeltic Watersports Festival
Liskeard & District Agricultural Show
Looe Lions Carnival Week
Padstow Vintage Rally
Pendeen Band Week
Perranporth Carnival
Porthleven Lifeboat Day
Ruan Minor Vintage Car Rally
Rock Sailing Club. Shrimper Week
St Endellion Music

July (continued)
St Germans. Port Eliot Literary Festival
St Mawes Regatta
Stithians Show
Tremough. Celtic Congress
Wadebridge Wheels

August
Bude Carnival
Bude Horticultural Show
Camel Sailing Week
Camelford Agricultural Show
Cornwall Folk Festival
Crying the Neck
Delabole Wind Fair
Falmouth Week
Fowey Royal Regatta & Carnival Week
Hayle Festival
Henri-Lloyd Falmouth Week
Mount Edgcumbe. Classic Car Rally & Fayre
Morvah Pasty Day Festival
Morval Vintage Steam Rally
Newlyn Fish Festival
Newquay. Rip Curl Boardmasters
Padstow Carnival
Padstow Lifeboat Day
Polruan Regatta
St Agnes Festival
St Keverne Ox St Just Feast
Wadebridge Carnival

September
Bude Jazz Festival
Truro. Cornish Food & Drink Festival
Looe Valley Walking Festival
Penzance. Open Gorseth
St Ives Festival

October
Boscastle. Food, Arts & Crafts Festival
Falmouth Oyster Festival
Perranporth. Lowender Peran

November
Falmouth & Penryn. Cornwall Film Festival
Looe Food Festival
Roseland Festival
Wadebridge Prime Stock Show

December
Padstow Christmas Festival
Mousehole. Tom Bawcock's Eve

For specific dates please contact the
local Tourist Information Centre